The Brown Batallions

Hitler's SA in Words and Pictures

Translated and Edited by
Nicholas H. Hatch

TURNER PUBLISHING COMPANY
Paducah, Kentucky

TURNER PUBLISHING COMPANY
Publishers of America's History
412 Broadway•P.O. Box 3101
Paducah, Kentucky 42002-3101
(270) 443-0121

Translated and Edited by
Nicholas H. Hatch

Publishing Consultant: Douglas W. Sikes

Library of Congress Catalog No. 97-00-103604
ISBN: 1-56311-596-6
LIMITED EDITION
Printed in the U.S.A.

FOREWORD

So many years ago that I've lost track, at some forgotten militaria or gun show in a city whose name I can no longer recall, I acquired the book you now hold in your hands in its original German form. It may have been purchased outright or it might have been part of a large trade deal with a fellow collector, but regardless of the circumstances of its acquisition, this book, which describes the SA's role in the rise of the National Socialist German Worker's Party and its final assumption of power, stirred an interest within me that I had no idea existed at that time - and led to this reprinting in English.

I was (and am) an ardent student of World War II history. Fascinated in my youth by war stories from family members and friends, I developed a passion for the subject that continues to this day. It still amazes my wife and children how I can sit through hours of endless movies and documentaries, or read and re-read countless books on World War II. As I am frequently reminded, "You know how it ends."

That is exactly what I found so interesting in this book. Although I had studied what I felt was just about every aspect of the war and the historical events that led up to it, I had personally never found many reference books on the founding and rise of the Party written from the "insider's" view.

That is the basis of this volume. It appeared in 1938 as an official publication of the SA. Written by SA members and loaded with dozens and dozens of interesting photographs, it is actually a complete history of the SA up to that time. But as many of you know, and hopefully others will learn, the story of the SA's beginnings and growth and that of the NSDAP are virtually one and the same. And it is the telling of that story by the SA men themselves that will interest you, as it did me. They were there at the beginning as protection during speeches and at Party gatherings. They were there when street fights and brawls with their opponents were everyday occurrences. They were there at the "Feldherrnhalle" in Munich on November 9, 1923 when they, their Party, and their Führer were stopped in the attempt to wrench the reins of government out of the hands of the "November criminals" as they referred to those that they felt "stabbed Germany in the back" with the armistice that Germany signed to end the first World War. They were there at the re-emergence of the Party and their own re-birth. They were there on the night of January 30, 1933 when their Führer finally reached the goal he had set for himself and his Party. And finally, they were there through the years up to 1938 and the original publication of this book. Not just as observers and casual witnesses of the struggles, victories and defeats of the men and the ideology that swept over Germany in the 1920's and early 1930's ending in the founding of the Third Reich, but actual participants in the making of history. For although the Party and Adolf Hitler existed first, they would never have risen to assume power in Germany without the SA. Hitler himself lets you know that at the front of this book.

One of the most frequently asked questions in the study of history is "why?". In reading this volume you will hopefully gain new insight into why the men of the SA were so completely devoted to Adolf Hitler and his philosophy and why thousands upon thousands of civilized, intelligent men helped lead one of the most culturally advanced countries in the world to catastrophic ruin by 1945.

An attempt has been made to put this book into a more readable form for those of us who speak English. The German language, for most of us, is not easy to follow, basically because of sentence structure. Added to this was the fact that it was written in a very heavy-handed, politically slanted style. Every attempt has been made to keep the content as true to the original German text as possible. The only additions made are a list of SA ranks and their approximate American counterparts, along with a description of the unit compositions regarding the number of men involved.

Over two hundred photos help make this book a pictorial as well as written history of the SA up to 1938. These photographs should be of special interest to collectors of SA uniforms, insignia and edged weapons.

When translating a work of this type from one language to another, there are bound to be some inaccuracies. If the reader identifies some misinformation in this book which needs to be brought to my attention, I welcome any input that can be documented and corrected in future works.

In any event, I hope the reader will find it as educational and entertaining as I have.

Nicholas H. Hatch
Doniphan, Missouri
September, 1999

ACKNOWLEDGMENTS

I owe a deep debt of gratitude to the following people for their assistance in the completion of this book: My wife, Sharon, for her endless hours of transcription, assistance in editing, and patience; and Connie Hawkinberry and Clint Morton for their assistance in translation.

PRE-WAR SA RANKS AND THEIR EQUIVALENTS

RANK	TRANSLATION	AMERICAN RANK
SA Mann	SA Man	Private
Sturmmann	Trooper	Private 1st Class
Rottenführer	Troop Leader	Corporal
Scharführer	Squad Leader	Corporal
Oberscharführer	Senior Section Leader	Sergeant
Truppführer	Platoon Leader	Staff Sergeant
Obertruppführer	Senior Troop Leader	Master Sergeant
Sturmführer	Company Leader	Second Lieutenant
Obersturmführer	Senior Company Leader	First Lieutenant
Sturmhauptfuhrer	Chief Company Leader	Captain
Sturmbannführer	Battalion Leader	Major
Obersturmbannführer	Senior Battalion Leader	Lt. Colonel
Standartenführer	Regiment Leader	Colonel
Oberführer	Chief Leader	Colonel
Brigadeführer	Brigade Division Leader	Brigadier General
Gruppenführer	Division Leader	Major General
Obergruppenführer	Senior Gruppe Leader	Lt. General
SA Stabschef	Chief of Staff	General

SA UNITS

GERMAN	MILITARY EQUIVALENT	UNIT COMPOSITION
Schar	Squad	8-16 Men
Trupp	Platoon	3-4 Scharen
Sturm	Company	3-4 Truppen
Sturmbann	Battalion	3-5 Sturm
Standarte	Regiment	3-5 Sturmbann
Brigade	Brigade	3-9 Standarten
Gruppe	Division	2-7 Brigades

„Alles, was ihr seid, seid ihr durch mich, und alles, was ich bin, bin ich nur durch euch allein!"

DER FÜHRER ZU SEINER SA. AM 30. 1. 1936

"Everything, what you are, you are through me and everything, what I am, I am only through you!"

The Führer to his SA on January 30, 1936.

The Führer to his SA on January 30, 1936.

HONOR BOARD
The Murder Victims of the Movement

1923

Felix Allfarth, November 9, Münich / Andreas Bauriedl, November 9, Münich / Theodor Casella, November 9, Münich / Wilhelm Ehrlich, 9. November, Münich / Martin Faust, November 9, Münich / Anton Hechenberger, November 9, Münich / Oskar Körner, November 9, Münich / Karl Kuhn, November 9, Münich / Karl LaForce, November 9, Münich / Kurt Neubauer, November 9, Münich / Klaus Von Pape, November 9, Münich / Theodor Von Der Pfordten, November 9, Münich / Hans Rickmers, November 9, Münich / Max Erwin Von Scheubner-Richter, November 9, Münich / Lorenz Ritter Von Stransky, November 9, Münich / Wilhelm Wolf, November 9, Münich / Karl Winter, February 26, Steinen / Daniel Sauer, May 1, Sickershausen / Albert Leo Schlageter, May 26, Düsseldorf / Ludwig Knickmann, June 21, Buer / Erich Kunze, September 24, Podelwitz / Dietrich Eckart, December 26, Berchtesgaden

1924

Rudolf Eck, March 5, Gehren / Willi Dreyer, March 21, Berlin / Rudolf Von Henke, July 1, Hindenburg / Friedrich Just, September 20, Roggenstorf / Artur Prack, December 5, Waldfischbach

1925

Fritz Kröber, April 26, Durlach / Matthias Mann, June 28, Rosenheim / Werner Doelle, August 9, Berlin

1926

Fritz Renz, February 21, Altlandsberg / Franz Kortyka, June 8, Miechowitz / Harry Anderssen, September 26, Berlin / Emil Müller, September 27, Germersheim

1927

Otto Senft, February 13, Dortmund / Wilhelm Wilhemi, March 6, Nastätten / Karl Ludwig, April 10, Wiesbaden / Georg Hirschmann, May 26, Münich / Eugen Eichhorn, September 11, Oelsnitz

1928

Bernhard Gerwert, April 19, Sythen / Gottfried Thomae, April 28, Essen / Heinrich Wölfel, May 2, Nuremberg / Heinrich Kottmann, May 13, Pfungstadt / Hans Kütemeyer, November 17, Berlin

1929

Heinrich Limbach, February 8, Podelwitz / Hermann Schmidt, March 7, Wöhrden / Otto Streibel, March 7, Wöhrden / Katharina Grünewald, August 2, Nuremberg / Erich Jost, August 5, Nuremberg / Heinrich Bauschen, October 19, Duisburg / Karl Rummer, October 20, Scwarzenbach / Gerhard Weber, November 4, Berlin / Friedrich Meier, December 8, Kyritz / Walter Fischer, December 14, Berlin

1930

Horst Wessel, February 23, Berlin / Edmund Behnke, March 16, Berlin / Kurt Günther, March 16, Chemnitz / Franz Engel, May 12, Stargard / Heinrich Messerschmitt, July 27, Kassel /Adalbert Schwarz, August 3, Vienna / Günther Wolf, August 3, Beuthen / Karl Paas, August 9, Haan / Heinrich Dreckmann, September 7, Hamburg / Heinz Ötting, September 11, Essen / Hans Kiessling, September 13, Schwarzenbach / Karl Taube, October 18, Rosenberg / Josef Hilmerich, November 21, Düsseldorf / Theodor Sanders, December 4, Hagen / Adolf Höh, December 7, Dortmund / Klaus Clemens, December 18, Bonn / Julius Hollmann, December 22, W. Barmen

1931

Ernst Weinstein, January 1, Stuttgart / Paul Thewellis, January 23, Düren / Richard Selinger, January 30, Niesky / Gerhard Bischoff, February 28, Steinseifersdorf / Fritz Felgendreher, March 14, Essen / Adolf Gerstenberger, March 16, Karlsmarkt / Karl Broeske, March 30, Dinslaken / Josef Felzen, March 30, Wittlich / Karl Freyburger, April 27, Deutscheylau / Fritz Tschierse, May 23, Königsberg / Paul Billet, May 25, Karlsruhe / Gerhard Liebsch, May 26, Dühringshof / Heinrich Gutsche, June 7, Chemnitz / Edgar Steinbach, June 7, Chemnitz / Josef Weber, June 16, Ebersberg / Edgar Müller, June 19, Neisse / Johann Gossel, June 21, Bremen / Walter Blümel, July 2, Leipzig / August Sievert, July 2, Peine / Karl Fiedler, July 6, Crossen / Hans Kersten, July 18, Uenze / Bruno Schaffrinski, July 20, Pollwitten / Alfred Rühmling, August 2, Wittstock / Herbert Grobe, August 15, Limbach / Hans Hoffmann, August 17, Berlin / Johannes Mallon, September 3, Bergen / Karl Bobis, September 4, Düsseldorf / Hermann Thielsch, September 9, Berlin / Gustav Seidlitz, September 20, Meseritz / Erich Garthe, October 6, Essen / Kurt Nowack, October 11, Berlin / Heinrich Böwe, October 18, Berlin / Max Gohla, October 29, Paulsdorf / Albert Müller, November 1, Remscheid / Erwin Moritz, November 5, Berlin / Wilhelm Decker, November 9, Bremen / Karl Radke, November 9, Eutin / Martin Martens, November 11, Neumünster / Walter Thriemer, November 11, Lugau / Horst Hoffmann, November 15, Kahlbude / Hans Hobelsberger, November 17, Worms / Egidius Geurten, November 20, Aachen

1932

Kurt Wietfeld, January 1, Völpke / Franz Czernuch, January 9, Hindenburg / Richard Menzel, January 10, Rendsburg / Arnold Guse, January 19, Essen / Ernst Schwartz, January 19, Berlin / Bruno Schramm, January 23, Zülz / Herbert Norkus, January 24, Berlin / Fritz Beubler, February 4, Nägelstedt / Georg Preiser, February 7, Berlin / Arno Kalweit, February 8, Kraupischken / Hans Karner, February 8, Schützen / Heinrich Heissinger, February, Hamburg / Walter Gornatowski, February 17, Klein-Gaglow / Franz Becker, February 20, Saarau / Wilhelm Sengotta, February 20, Massen / Artur Wiegels, February 22, Schwinde / August Brackmann, February 29, Tessin / Otto Ludwig, March 6, Berlin / Willi Thielsch, March 8, Breslau / Karl Panke, March 11, Bobersberg / Erich Jaenecke, March 14, Gardelegen / Max Beulich, April 4, Mittweida / Ludwig Frisch, April 8, Chemnitz / Friedrich Hellmann, April 8, Berlin / Heinz Brands, April 10, Hamburg / Harry Hahn, April 10, Hamburg / Silvester Gratzl, April 17, St. Andrae /Johann Broweleit, April 23, Hamborn / Johann Lüchtenborg, April 23, Harkebrügge / Udo Curth, April 24, Berlin / Paul Stenzhorn, May 5, Oberhausen / Silvester Fink, May 27, Innsbruck / Jodoc Kehrer, May 31, Burscheid / Emil Erich Fröse, June 3, Lünen / Hans Hilbert, June 19, W.-Barmen / Wilhelm Hambückers, June 20, Uebach / Kurt Hilmer, June 20, Erkrath / Helmut Köster, June 22, Berlin / Heinrich Habenicht, June 23, Dortmund / Fritz Borawski, June 26, Wattenscheid / Werner Gerhardt, June 30, Zeitz / Hermann Zapp, June 30, Kaiserslautern / Hans Steinberg, July 1, Berlin / Friedrich Karpinski, July 2, Essen / Hans Handwerk, July 5, Frankfurt / Walter Ufer, July 5, Dortmund / Ludwig Decker, July 10, Beverungen / Georg Konjetzke, July 10, Ohlau / Herbert Stanetzki, July 10, Ohlau / Heinrich Grasmeher, July 11, Steeden / Kurt Kreth, July 12, Köslin / Günther Ross, July 12, Köslin / Fritz Schröder, July 17, Berlin / Ulrich Massow, July 17,

Greifswald / Bruno Reinhard, July 17, Greifswald / Herbert Schuhmacher, July 17, Greifswald / Helene Winkler, July 17, Altona / Heinrich Koch, July 17, Altona / Peter Büddig, July 18, Altona / Herbert Härtel, July 18, Gross-Rosen / Robert Bitzer, July 27, Wiehl / Johann Raskin, July 28, Eilendorf / Erich Sallie, July 29, Wiederitzsch / Otto Reinke, July 30 Königsberg / Peter Kölln, July 31, Itzehoe / Fritz Schrön, July 31, Essen / Axel Schaffeld, August 1, Braunschweig / Johannes Reifegerste, August 3, Frohburg / Fritz Schulz, August 3, Berlin / Herbert Gatschke, August 30, Berlin / August Assmann, September 6, Graz / Josef Lass, September 7, Leoben / Gregor Schmid, October 10, Stuttgart / Alfred Kindler, October 16, Leipzig / Josef Staller, October 16, Vienna / Karl Heinzelmann, October 20, Hamburg / August Pfaff, October 22, Castrop / Helmut Barm, October 23, Bochum / Richard Harwick, October 27, Berlin / Heinrich Hammacher, November 3, Duisburg / Kurt Reppich, November 4, Berlin / Johann Cyranka, November 5, Hamburg / Oskar Mildner, November 7, Chemnitz / Erwin Jänisch, November 25, Berlin / Eduard Elbrächter, November 28, Brackwede / Ernst Bich, December 9, Barmen / Vinzenz Szczotok, December 25, Bottrop

1933

Walter Wagnitz, January 1, Berlin / Erich Sagasser, January 8, Berlin / Erich Stenzel, January 13, Berlin / Hans Bernsau, January 18, Jserlohn / Fritz Wetekam, January 20, Düsseldorf / Hans Maikowski, January 31, Berlin / Rudolf Brügmann, February 1, Lübeck / Josef Marcus, February 1, Homberg / Leopold Paffrath, February 1, Homberg / Karl Guwang, February 3, Sinsheim / Paul Passmann, February 5, Bochum / Friedrich Schreiber, February 5, Dormagen / Franz Cieslik, February 11, Hecklingen / Paul Berck, February 12, Eisleben / Franz Müller, February 15, Siegburg / Kurt V. D. aHe, February 19, Berlin / Gerhard Schlemminger, February 22, Berlin / Walter Spangenberg, February 25, Köln / Winand Winteberg, February 25, Köln / Otto Blöcker, February 26, Hamburg / Christian Crössmann, February 26, Lindenfels / Josef Bleser, February 28, Frankfurt / Eduard Felsen, February 28, Berlin / Josef Cibulski, March 1, Bochum / Julius Hoffmann, March 3, Düsseldorf / Andreas Weidt, March 3, Höchst / Friedrich Heine, March 4, Duisburg / Fritz Geisler, March 5, Breslau / Kurt Eckert, March 6, Berlin / Kurt Hausmann, March 6, Schönebeck / Franz Kopp, March 8, Berlin / Herbert Welkisch, March 8, Breslau / Gustav Lehmann, March 15, Schönebeck / Peter Friess, March 17, Lindenfels / Emil Trommer, March 17, Altona / Otto Schmelzer, April 4, Güdingen / Johannes Loch, April 29, Raudten / Franz Ertl, May 1, Altheim / Josef Wiesheier, May 21, Gaiganz / Heinrich Stollenwerk, May 28, Düsseldorf / Paul Ulrich, June 4, Düsseldorf / Matthias Schwarz, June 11, Miesenbach / Walter Apel, June 21, Berlin / Ronert Gleuel, June 22, Berlin / Wilhelm Klein, June 27, Berlin / Gerhard Landmann, June 29, Braunschweig / Paul Scholpp, August 14, Stuttgart / Wilhelm Koziollek, August 15, Wanne-Eickel / Alfred Manietta, October 1, Leipzig / Josef Woltmann, October 6, Buer-Erle / Walter Dokter, October 28, Maliers

1934

Erich Tessmer, May 13, Lünen / Kurt Elsholz, June 18, Gollmütz / Lorenz Serwazi, September 28, Köln / Gerhard Kauffmann, September 29, Berlin

1935

Ralph Baberadt, January 15., Hamburg / Martin Demmig, March 30, Breslau / Kurt Blankenberg, April 24, Wriezen / Kurt Flatzek, June 21, Mittweida

1936

Wilhelm Gustloff, February 4, Davos / Bernhard Schlothan, March 10, Wanne-Eickel / Franz Scotkiewicz, March 31, Peine / Ernst Ludwig, June 13, Danzig / Günther Deskowski, June 13, Danzig / Paul Fressonke, June 16, Danzig / Hans Hahner, July 19. Barcelona / Wilhelm Gätje, July 24, San Martin / Helmuth Hofmeister, July 24, San Martin / Günther Swalmius-Dato, July 24, San Martin / Thomas Treiz, July 24, San Martin / Heinz Voss, July 30, Gijon / Friedrich Lothar Güdde, November 11, Derio B. Bilbao / Julius Steininger, November 24, Duisburg-Meiderich

The 5th Company of the B Detachment of the SA Regiment Münich is marching home after an exercise in the year 1922.
B Detachment was the name for the Watch Company, consisting of senior members of the SA Regiment, which was under the command of Oberleutnant Brückner, currently SA Obergruppenführer and Adjutant of the Führer.

Political actions and events slip very quickly through the hands and hearts of those that experience them. No wonder that the generations that were not eye and ear witnesses of that time have only a weak memory to carry into the future when again and again narrow-minded people are once more captivated by new great events, achievements and creations which determine the picture of the day. It is the intellectual passions of researchers and inquiring minds not content with the descriptions and assessment of the facts which emanate from the records which causes them to trace the roots and rediscover and reconstruct what we call history.

Teachers and champions of history have not always fully agreed upon it, whether neutral, political

Left: A flag from the beginnings of the Movement in Northern Germany.
Hannover had the first local group of the NSDAP in Northern Germany. Founded July 2, 1921, the dedication of the banner took place in the great hall of the Hofbrauhaus in Münich on March 29, 1922.

Above: The armband of the 5th Company of the SA Regiment in Münich.
The number shown on the swastika denotes the company number, the star was the insignia of the leader.

Marching of the SA on the occasion of the consecration of the flag in Passau in the year 1922.
The SA still had their standard uniforms. Besides civilian clothing, they wore the honored gray uniform of the front solider.

researchers and finders of those strengths whose results we have in front of us as facts of the past. Even though it is necessary to answer the questions of historical methods and ways and to digest what we find, to deal with our minor but so important subjects, the narrowness of the scope forces us to be content with the modern directions of the historical research. National Socialism has eliminated any doubt that history is only of any value if the results of the historical research directly affect the political present, if the researcher realizes the value of his work and deciphers it for everyone else in the present. The new era is convinced that a value-free view of history can guide the people, or better yet a small minority, to romantic enthusiasm whose heroes easily

The SA on the march.
The year 1922 can be considered as the year of the gathering and focusing on the coming dispute. Here we see Münich SA men of the 17th Hundertschaft (group of 100) during a field exercise in Freimann, headed by the present SA Gruppenführer and Deputy Chief Editor of the "Völkischer Beobachter" ("People's Observer") Josef Berchtold (to the left), who was the commander of the "Stosstrupp Hitler", November 9, 1923.

The first large-scale deployment of the Sturmabteilung took place at the Marsfeld in Münich on the occasion of the Party Days (January 27-29, 1923).
Effectively protected by the SA, the Party thus was more and more in the lives of the people. The flags shown in the picture are the first Sturm flags of the SA. On that date they were dedicated along with the Standards.

accept offerings of disharmony and narrow-mindedness from the hands of slightly dull novices. Even though we are not greedy utilitarianists, we are not satisfied with neutral effects which just burden our minds. We would like to know: What would we learn from Heinrich the Lion, from Friedrich the Great, from Bismarck? What is engaging to us about the history of the SA, which is not even history yet, but the present whose farthest end is

Through prohibition and troubles.
In winter 1922-23 the trip to Regensburg planned by Sturmabteilung men was prohibited. The participants are leaving Münich's main train station and marching home.

The Day of Germany in Nuremberg in 1923 was a powerful rally of a united people's group under the leadership of the NSDAP.
In the picture we see, Julius Streicher, Gauleiter of Franken among the officers of the old army. The march past took place in the Adolf Hitler Platz, which received its name after the seizure of power, and is now the annual site of the impressive march past of the fighting organization of the NSDAP in front of the Führer on the occasion of the Reichs Party Days.

gradually disappearing from our view and becomes a domain of historical interest. A good example of the diversity of the SA is the fact that nobody ever asked how long it has existed.

What does a number mean?

It can only be of interest if it has been irrevocably lost in the depths of the memory of the past.

Certainly, a fighting adventure, the whole struggle, an injury to the body, a healing scar, and a few marching brown columns convey more than a date. Is it of importance to know that a fighting Trupp of the young National Socialist German Worker's Party, which was founded on August 3, 1921, became known as the "Sturmabteilung", the "SA", on October 5th and entered the political picture of the most recent present?

We only want to know that day because it was the beginning of the National Revolution which, with remarkable consequence, twelve years later had done all that it had planned to do. This idea should be the foundation on which we would like to build the fundamental parts of the history of the SA. Twelve years don't allow much room to include all the facts and events which a candidate who wants to pass a history exam has to know by heart. This is the reason why it is not difficult at all to place a description that meets all of the requirements of the exactness and factual interests in that attempt to comprehend and appreciate the history of the SA. Without any effort, the years themselves supply the sections of this calendar.

A picture of the Stosstrupp Hitler 1923.
Sitting above the cab top: Stosstruppführer Party Comrade Josef Berchtold, the present SA Gruppenführer, Deputy Chief Editor of the "Völkischer Beobachter" in München, and founder of the combat paper the "SA Mann". Third from the left in front with glasses: The chauffeur for many years and loyal friend of the Führer, Party Comrade Julius Schreck, who passed away May 16, 1936 due to his combat injuries.

HISTORY OF THE SA

We know that the Sturmabteilung of the NSDAP (National Socialist German Workers Party) was founded in the summer of 1921. It remains to be said that only a few months later, on November 4th of the same year, the young SA had its inauguration. At the Hofbrauhaus, 46 fanatical fighters challenged over 800 Marxists and did all they could to break up the meeting.

That act instantly put the young fighting Trupp on the political stage. The SA became a visible expression of the power of the fighting Party which represented the revolutionary goals of Adolf Hitler. A few men tried to swim against the current of the general political breakdown, the national despair and the public degeneracy. A concentration of the uniting forces had begun. Maybe this beginning was only a symbol at that time. In fact, it appeared to be a departure into a new era which actually would begin much later.

This era was so occupied with itself that it did not see the strength of the defense and the renovation. On the other hand, they had to become a power factor, a team, an irresistible force before they could declare war on Germany's enemies. Nevertheless, the second year of the SA became a time of organization and internal consolidation without missing an opportunity to speak and to deliver a blow to those who they would one day defeat.

The calendar for the year 1922 mentions some significant events whose results no one could have predicted. In early August the young SA celebrated its one year anniversary at the Burgerbraukeller in Münich. Just fourteen days later the first marching columns demonstrated under waving swastika flags, together with the patriotic groups of Münich, against the Protection Law of the Republic. Taking advantage of this opportunity, the men of the SA won the right to the street against a much larger majority of Marxists.

In September it proved useful to consolidate the SA of Münich and the SA of the provincial towns of the present NSDAP districts to eight Hundredschaften (groups of 100), which increased constantly. On November 23rd the 11th Hundredschaften was organized, consisting mainly of students under the command of Rudolf Hess.

Münich had become too small for the action base of the Party and its brown guard. On October 14 and 15, Adolf Hitler traveled to Coburg on the occasion of the Day of Germany. This first marching day of the NSDAP has been reconstructed and described many times from the memories of the marchers. We would only like to mention that the Coburg Day was the Day of the SA, a presentation of the troops of young forces which prompted a decision concerning the struggle of the Party.

The decision was closer than expected. The year 1923 accelerated the breakdown of the destroyed German Nation like the force of an avalanche. The French invaded the region around the Ruhr River; the particular forces split up; it looked like the destiny of the German people had been determined.

On the day of the National Revolt.
Loading of Hitler's raiding parties on the morning of November 9, 1923, prior to the arrest of the red City Council in Münich. The consequence was the march which found its tragic end at the "Feldherrnhalle" with the sacrificial death of the first sixteen martyrs of the Movement.

The winterstorm blew the worthless leaves of the growing inflation and drew a chaotic picture of this German era.

In the last days of January, the avant-garde of the NSDAP marched on the Marsfeld in Münich on the first Reichspartietag ("Reichs Party Day"). Almost untouched by the threatening decisions of the tribunal of the breakdown, a new force constituted itself to which Adolf Hitler dedicated the first four field insignia. As a note, we would like to mention that at that time the first Sturm banner outside of this area had been sent to Zwickau to the heart of the red Saxons.

A few days later the SA formed a union with other fighting groups which consolidated the leadership of the Sturmabteilung in the task force of the patriotic fighting groups. In March, Hermann Göring, the last leader of the Richthofenstaffel (Richtofen Squadron), was assigned as SA Commander and Führer of all of the Sturmabteilung. Oberleutnant Brückner took over the command of the SA Regiments in Münich at the same time.

While everything urged that a decision be made, the SA prepared itself for its last mission. Major exercises in Forstenrieder Park and near Freimann shortly afterwards precluded the armed march of the entire Bavarian SA and other fighting units at the Oberwiesenfeld.

At the Oberwiesenfeld in Münich on May 1, 1923.
The spirit of the SA was created according to the Führer's will out of the lost days of earlier senseless class-struggles and demonstrations, the strength of the work of a united people.

The national involvement of the Police and Reichswehr delayed the final argument and conflict one more time.

November 8th arrived. At the hour in question the Führer put his entire power and the destiny of the young Movement on the scales. The young guards were destroyed by the beatings of the traitors. However, Germany was safe. Hermann Göring was among those brought down in the fire of the machine guns of the enemy. He was severely wounded and fled to Austria.

The Führer was arrested. The head of the Party was missing in the worst hours following the first revolution on November 8th and 9th. Most loyal co-fighters and comrades of Adolf Hitler tried to save what they could. Further existence of the SA was illegal and the return of Adolf Hitler was not expected. The Party was re-established in 1925 by the strong support of and steps by the old SA beside Adolf Hitler.

What are the names in the history of this organization in which each individual mastered each difficult task with a lot of courage and unselfishness? The chroniclers won't be able to pass over the men who were always there when they did more than they were supposed to do. There is Oberleutnant Kriebel, there is Joseph Berchtold, the Führer of Hitler's Stosstrupp, the first Reichsführer of the **SS**, one of Adolf Hitler's closest co-workers in the times of the decisions. The Party lives again.

At the top you will find the SA. With this the

power and the significance of the National Socialistic Movement grew. Beyond the central events of the Reichs Party Days in the years 1926, 1927 and 1929 decisions were made, there were victories and struggles which formed whole calendars which cannot be numbered. However their meaning has become the guidelines of the entire German Nation. Certainly at that time Adolf Hitler was the Party and the Party was Adolf Hitler. The political power branch represented the daily involvement of the double terms "Führer" and "Party", this was the SA in those days.

Does anybody believe that the people would have noticed and been interested in the rabble-rousing speeches of the small National Socialistic Reichstag faction when nothing but the march steps and the fighting songs of the SA Stürme set the beat of the reality of a relentless critic and a parliamentarian revenge with the true enemies of the German Nation? There was a time when the press of the opponents of the young Movement was silent concerning things which would have received the attention of the public, the consequences of the weight of the arguments, and of the validity of the critical thoughts. There was a time when no paper even mentioned a word about the Reichstag speeches of the pioneers of the Party.

During that time the SA was marching into the bullets of the Communist agitators. At that time students and the unemployed broke down under the truncheon of the Republic. At that time drummer korps in brown uniforms were chasing disinterested citizens out of their beds and gathered friends and enemies from the curbs during their marches for Germany. The assault parties of

One room where history was made.
The branch office of the NSDAP in the Schellingstrasse in Münich from the beginnings of the Movement. From left to right, the Party Comrades: Kassenwart (Treasurer) Schwarz, SA Führer von Pfeffer, Geschäftsführer (Managing Secretary) Bouhler.

A typical picture from the time of struggle.
Away from all civilian conveniences, SA men with their Sturm banner went to the rallies, always vigilant and ready to make sacrifices for the important goal of the Führer. Second from the left: Party Comrade Brückner, the present Adjutant of the Führer.

March of the National Socialistic fighting groups to the roll call on the occasion of the Day of Germany in Halle on May 11, 1924.
Next to the SA, marching on this day were the Reichskriegsflagge, Frontbann, Bund Oberland, and many other national units for the unification of the German people. At that time the Führer was still at the fortress in Landsberg.

the SA could not be killed and you could not ignore them either. They were a live agitation walking through towns and villages demonstrating for the Movement, which assured them a place in public opinion.

Who are these young men? What does this political union want? Why do these suicide candidates provoke the terror of the Red Front?

For months these questions had only been a preliminary echo of the considerable involvement of the Sturmabteilung of the NSDAP. Each march increased the general uncertainty. In the parliaments of the land and in the communes, the representatives of the growing Party increased the interest of the aroused public.

The Party could no longer be kept silent. The Party marched in SA columns, visible to everybody, which caused a lot of deaths. The threatened enemies had to use desperate measures.

With each battle the brown convoys of the German Revolution became stronger than before. Mutual need, mutual dangers, one single strong idea linked the men. In them, the Party was on the attack. The leadership of the National Socialist Movement dictated the law of action to their opponents.

Happy little islands in the flood of terror and persecution were the Party

Days of the NSDAP. Who was surprised by the fact that these days above all were true presentations of the Sturmabteilungen? In Weimar, in Nuremberg, and again in Nuremberg, they were marching in tens of thousands and showed to the world an example of their power and their will, and gained the power to hold on to fight during the losing battle on which they had placed the idea and the command of their hearts.

Every old SA man recalls with pleasure those little SA gatherings which seem to be kind of an echo of the major recurrent troop presentations. Each Sunday pried each man from his home, from his family, from his well-deserved rest, to a new action on the front.

District marches, meetings and demonstrations didn't allow time for people to have any rest. From the truck convoys the SA men shouted "Deutschland Erwache" (Germany, wake up) throughout the towns and areas. For each dead man, ten new ones jumped in who yesterday were still Communists or ignorant citizens. The SA was already a state within the State; a piece of future in the sad present; an omen of the new era before the troubles of a sinking era.

Only by writing about the history of the SA will the adventures of the time of struggle be known to the present generation.

The Führer at the front of the propaganda marches during the Party Days in Weimar on July 3 and 4, 1926.
Next to the Führer, Generalleütnant (Lieutenant General) a. D. (Retired) Heinemann. In the middle, SA Obergruppenführer Schwarz, Treasurer of the NSDAP. To the right, Reichsleiter Alfred Rosenberg.

The Führer and his SA on the occasion of the Reichs Party Days in Weimar, July 3 and 4, 1926.
To the right, behind the Führer, former Gausturmführer (District Storm Leader) of the Ruhr District and present Stabschef (Chief of Staff) Lutze. These rallies were during the time the Führer was prohibited to speak, which was canceled in Spring, 1927.

The SA in Weimar in 1926.
Standarte (standard) and sturmfahne (storm flag), always sacred symbols of the fighter. In front, the Bavarian SA Gruppe, among them war veteran and invalid, blind and armless Rudi Jungmayr, (X), who has been marching with the Blutordensträger (Blood Order holders) in the München SA.

March through Weimar in the year 1926.
The conqueror of Berlin, Party Comrade Dr. Goebbels, at that time Geschäftsführer of the District Rhein-Ruhr, and Gausturmführer Party Comrade Lutze, the present Stabschef, at the front of the procession of brown shirts.

Sometimes we who marched in the Ruhr District remember that we were afraid from one march to the other and from one meeting to the other, which we have now nearly forgotten. In the hidden spots of our convictions there is only a high feeling left, which we guard like a treasure.

Will we ever be able to mobilize it for those who will be our new comrades today and tomorrow? The economic situation has taken hold of our memories and molded them in any form possible, as well as marketed them. The State and the Party have shouted "stop" to the profit makers.

In any event, the willingness to participate in the idea of the time of struggle has disgusted many. Maybe it would have been best to wait for a new, more favorable moment in which the chosen one gave the big adventure of the fighting SA, in suitable ways, to those who participate in the fruits of our victory.

The year 1929 came to an end in sight of the powerful Nuremberg demonstration. Where was the time? For how long would we have to march before the morning of victory dawned? The election in September, 1930 put an end to all doubts of our opponents. The NSDAP advanced to become the second largest party.

The SA increased to be the most powerful fighting troop against the crumbling Republic. No sacrifice remained to be given. The raging defense of the enemies broke the most hopeful lives. Over the graves of the dead comrades stormed onward the unstoppable columns of the Revolution. No torment, no paragraph, no prohibition stopped the onward march. With nearly 300 dead, the triumphant SA

After the cancellation of the prohibition to speak in Bavaria on March 5, 1927.
Adolf Hitler gives a speech in the Luitpold Arena on the occasion of the Reichs Party Day in Nuremberg on August 21, 1927. As always, the Party Day was the highlight of the great march to freedom during the time of struggle.

The Münich SA Sturm 5 on the occasion of a propaganda tour at Tegernsee in the year 1927.
The old SA brought the Führer's ideas to each house in the most distant villages in Bavaria.

marched in rows through the Brandenburg Gate in the hour of the takeover on January 30, 1933.

We all, the old SA and the young comrades among us, have entered a new work phase which is different than during the time of struggle. The SA in the new State, this is a political reality which is strongly vivid over all temporary crises.

It is not totally up to us to honor the presence of our fighting formations. We have the time to wait for the judgment of those who come after us. One thing seems to be worth saying to end this contemplation, the old SA and its full battalions will keep on marching for the goals which we were dedicated to achieve in an era when the outcome did not look profitable. As certain as the Party, it will be the basis of the history of the National Socialistic Germany. That is our reward!

Election propaganda tour of the Bavarian SA in 1928.
In the car to the front right is Hans Schemm, Gauleiter of the Bavarian Ostmark and Bavarian Minister of Education,
who had a fatal accident on March 5, 1935. His last SA rank was Gruppenführer.

The Reichs Party Days in Nuremberg August 1–4, 1929.
Marching of the SA in front of the Führer.

The hospital transfer ticket from a Berlin emergency room where SA Sturmführer Horst Wessel, who was wounded during the war for independence for Germany, passed away on February 23, 1930.

A document, a piece of history.

Only this must be said: the present and future work of the SA is political involvement. The State's definition can be expressed in a little formula which makes the SA man a political soldier. Maybe the meaning of this work will become clear when projected to a comparatively separate new and past meaning of the State. In as little as the new State still is a night watch institution to procure independent and uninhibited individual involvement, the political soldier is the active State-related people's comrade, part of the new political unit which will shape the Nation, rather than the public concerns from a homogeneous mass of individuals.

From the fight for Berlin in 1930.
National Socialistic mass rally at the Sportpalast. The uniform prohibition of the government system forced the SA to appear in white shirts.

Also a certificate.
These so-called "identity cards" had to be issued numerously during the uniform prohibition time.

The involvement of the political army formed by the SA is both jointly and individually tenacious. It is clear that each political development involves a physical transition period and interpretation. Past such necessary situations remains the important tasks of the political team which, for the future, realizes where the essential value of people and State lies and encourages them. This requires some explanation. The present supplies us generously and forcefully.

The actual fighting area of the political soldier is the same as those mental conflicts imposed on the men of the present by the National Socialistic revolt.

The political soldier is ruled by discipline and a belief that he is the loyal friend and the sword of a political leadership which makes the basic feelings of the people and the race become reality. Nothing can resist the legal invasion of the new and powerful champions.

....with steady firm pace.
Despite the red terror, the SA marches through the streets of Spandau in the summer of 1932 with the SA men who were injured by the opponents during the daily sacrificial involvement at the front. The time of struggle before taking over power made the opponents take long strides toward efforts to prevent the approaching victory of the Movement by all, though frequently very shoddy, methods.

Active spirit of the victims. SA Mann Hemmerling from SZ I/18 Neustadt-Haardt, who had been severely injured by rivals during the march of 8,000 SA men in the summer of 1932.

I had a comrade. Funeral ceremony at the Berlin Wallstrasse for SA Sturmführer Maikowski, who was assassinated on his way home after the historic torchlight parade on the night of January 30, 1933.

Drawing by Elk Eber.

The historical torchlight procession of the SA in Berlin on Monday, January 30, 1933.
The day of the assumption of power through the Führer and Reichs Chancellor Adolf Hitler brought a fateful turn for the German Nation. "We assume our duties freely", the Führer said in those days, and he has kept his word. The homage of the brown columns before Supreme SA Führer Adolf Hitler in these historic hours was a symbol of the unbreakable vow of loyalty that was the active profession of faith to the construction of the Third Reich – The SA always marches in the front of the front lines on the side of the Führer.

Freie Wahl in Deutschland

This is how the journalists saw the sacrificial involvement of the SA for the entertainment of the German people.

TRANSLATION OF CARTOONS
Left Cartoon:
Top: Free Elections in Germany
Left door: Application Slips For Concentration Camp
Right door: Polling Station
Below: Everybody voting "Yes" enter here— Everybody voting "No", the other entrance, march!

Lower left cartoon:
Top: Cold Life
Below: Hey, is this still where you can get work?

Lower center cartoon:
Beside soldier: Beautiful uniform and big mouth.
Below: These are the characteristics of the National Socialist heroes. Women and young people have on September 14th an essential percentage of the angry National Socialist voices. They are the suggestion force of the toned down phrases, the inferior military drill. They know neither the Party program nor other essential publications of the swastika. They only know that the National Socialists promised mountains of gold. Many meanwhile already recognize that this gold is still less gold than that of the alchemist's thousand. Far too many women however still run with blindfolded eyes through the world. Help now comrade to enlighten these voters! The International Woman's Day is a valid fight against fascism, for socialism! So thanks, when you meet acquaintances! Did you already recruit the second comrade?

Lower Right Cartoon:
Top: The Free Speech
Newspaper annoucement: National Socialist Loepelmann, Court Minister a.D. , said that the "Jew bastard" name caller will be absolved. "In the expressions 'bastard', 'cow dung' and 'scoundrel' that the defendant called the minister, the court is unable to see any insult. Such language quite corresponds to the mind of the court of justice."

In the Revolver-Gazetten newspaper of the post-war era, the young National Socialistic Movement was not treated fairly with ink, pen and paper and the SA always appeared unwanted. The brown outfit of the SA men was the symbol for all hated political opposition of the red heroes on the bitter drawing table and, if you had a chance to take revenge on this opponent with artistic methods, then

A well-known tactic.
A treacherous attack of the Commune on an SA pub and already some Marxist paper turns the facts the other way around.

Right: "Education" appeal to the women.

In the service of justice.
The acquittal of an SA man made the Jewish papers stir up hatred against those judges who were not intimidated during the System era.

They were not inspired by enthusiasm.
According to the drawing of the artist, spontaneous and cordial rallies of the masses of people on January 30, 1933 and later, were apparently rehearsed as a mass chorus.

That's what the responses to our speakers looked like.
The practice of Jewish scribblers underlines their own SA statistics. The percentage of criminals among these November people might have been higher than 25%.

be a tolerant newspaper and had to take an even more tolerant road.

Of course, the permanent favorite hobby of the SA man in these pictures was always to deal with destroyed room furnishings, blood-dripping daggers and beautiful uniforms, not to mention their "big mouths". Otherwise, they developed a striking preference for half-open back doors and cracked windowpanes, and generally acted liked skilled criminals in public and at the court, and above all had the task to force the voters into being yes sayers and concentration camp candidates, with or without the use of large-caliber Brownings and gallows detention. So this is the way the SA conquered the new empire? But the question of the sane human mind and effect created by the SA itself speaks a clearer language than any of the misused newspaper pages and drawing tables. Accordingly, we can go to the next page on the agenda smiling understandingly.

Another method of turning things around.
The legal way to power strictly prescribed by the Führer in the time of struggle was very difficult for the opponents because the challenges would take cold blood. The defense of the SA in self-defense situations was turned into added attacks by the journalists.

The romantic environment.
What it looked like in the underworld clubs of their own followers and supporters so represented for the Novemberlings and Commune, the SA homes. They could not imagine a human society without killing tools and deceit.

TRANSLATION OF CARTOONS

Upper Left Cartoon:
Top: The Scream
Tablet: We are given orders by Adolf Hitler to scream enthusiastically.
Below: People listen! We are practicing: all short and enthusiastic scream.
Attention, scream out: - "Ha!!!"

Upper Right Cartoon:
Top: ....as the practice proves!
Tablet: 25% of the SA are pre-tried as criminals for theft, embezzlement or sex crimes.
Lower: "All criminals are Marxists!"

Lower Left Cartoon:
Top: The camouflage cap of the SA.

Lower Right Cartoon:
Top: The "Innocent" Nazi homes.
Sign: The simple knuckle duster.
Lower: "— and when the police come, we sing a cheerful song."

The Stabschef with his loved ones.
The Stabschef's job requires long journeys throughout the whole year. This family shares the destiny of so many whose head is wearing the brown shirt by living without the spouse and father in the interest of the Movement.

Among the leading personalities who nowadays are in responsible positions of the National Socialist empire and fight, the Stabschef of the SA has an outstanding position. Viktor Lutze is one of those who came home to the German homeland in a favorable situation after the World War. It is no coincidence that the first fighters of Adolf Hitler came from the rows of those soldiers who had been spared by the war and who were looking for a new future in the ruins of a broken empire. German democracy has never been their friend. In the interim empire of the Weimar Republic, the soldiers found the new homeland with the best virtues of the German man....honor, courage, love for the homeland.... despised, impaired and trampled on. When the Führer called these fighters, he gave them a new symbol and a new belief and they saw a way out of the desperation of the time. Adolf Hitler awoke the old virtues of the German soldier again. That's why soldiers and officers of the old troops are among his co-fighters.

The way of life for the Stabschef is turning a soldier into a political fighter.

"Taken September 5, 1923"
is written on the back of the photograph. It shows the young activist Lutze who had returned from the very front of the horrendous struggling of the nations unbroken. At that time he already was completely devoted to Adolf Hitler's ideas.

Stabschef Lutze was born in Bevergern, Westfalen on December 28, 1890. He served his military time as a first year cadet. In the beginning of the war he joined the 369th Infantry Regiment and later RES Infantry Regiment 15. In 1919 he was dismissed due to an eye injury. Soon after that he started a commercial courier business which he practiced in Elberfeld. There he soon came in touch with the NSDAP whose member he became in 1922. As SA Führer he actively got involved in the Ruhr defense in 1923. In 1925 he was appointed as leader of the "Gausturm" in the Ruhr Gau. Using his own ideas he designed the new organization and service badges for the SA units. One year later he became Führer of the SA for the Ruhr Gau and at the same time Deputy Gauleiter.

With steel helmet, gas mask and walking stick.
— an indispensable tool in frequently plowed-through areas — stands Lutze in field gray at the very front of the trench.

"First year" Viktor Lutze. Here you see "first year" Viktor Lutze at Munster Camp in H. in 1913.

Beginning 1926.
The SA Gauleiter of the Ruhr, Lutze, with his "hundertschaften" on the occasion of a propaganda march in Hattingen in the Ruhr. Only SA Gauleiter Lutze was wearing the brown shirt and the field-gray hat. The second from the left is present Führer of the Gruppe Sachsen, Obergruppenführer Schepmann.

Gau Tag (District Day) in Essen.
In April, 1927 thousands of comrades participated in the Gau meeting in Essen which had been called by Gau Sturmführer Lutze for his SA.

1931.
The Führer arrived to visit Oldenburg. To the left of the Führer is (at that time) Obergruppenführer Lutze, and behind them Rudolf Hess. To the right of the Führer is Obergruppenführer Herzog, Stabsführer of the SA High Command, who was the Führer of Untergruppe Weser-Ems at that time.

Highlights in the work of the Gruppen.
On the occasion of the annual big roll call, the Stabschef speaks to many tens of thousands of SA Führers and Mannern (men) in all Districts of Germany, always voicing to them Adolf Hitler's belief.

Very rarely, because of his voluminous work and high responsibility, does he take time for his favorite hobby, horseback riding.

The Stabschef and his family.
Most of the year the Stabschef travels by airplane, train and car, always at the front. The term "leisure time" is eliminated from the Stabschef's vocabulary. If he gets one hour for himself, then it will be spent with his family.

An autograph, please.
Everywhere when the Stabschef arrives, he is surrounded by young people. His signature under his picture is the ransom.

At all events, marches, etc. it is a great occasion when the Stabschef meets with a victim of the Great War. These men know that the Stabschef, who suffered severe wounds four times due to the great struggle of the Nation, has remained one of them.

Hunt in Spring, 1936.
Here you can see the Stabschef with the Reichsjägermeister (Master of the Hunt) of the Reich, Obergruppenführer Göring, on the occasion of a hunt, a hobby he can only practice very seldom due to his numerous duties.

The Stabschef as Oberpräsident.
Even in his position as Oberpräsident, the Stabschef takes care of all tasks related to all areas of his province. Here he visits the local museum at Stade.

the year 1930 he was appointed Supreme SA Führer Nord in annover and then in 1932 he was appointed Obergruppenführer for e Obergruppe West. Since 1930, Stabschef Lutze has been a member of the Reichstag. After the taking over of power, his political es were First President of the Province of Hannover and Police esident of the City of Hannover.

"You are the champions of the German Revolution!"
Week by week the Stabschef visits minor and major SA units and shows the means and ways of the SA struggles. These rallies with the Stabschef have always been a great experience for all of the men.

The Supreme SA Führer and his Stabschef.
The highlight of the Reichs Party Days is the appeal of the Führer to his SA at the Luitpold arena and seeing the brown battalions marching by. Every SA Mann will never forget the moment he feels Adolf Hitler's eyes looking at him and the Stabschef saluting his comrades.

Further, he was called to the Prussian State Court. In 1934, Supreme SA Führer Adolf Hitler appointed him as Stabschef.

So the soldier from Germany's years of embarrassment became a champion for national honor and independence, who from the first days of the Movement went the way of fights and sacrifices among Adolf Hitler's followers for the completion of the Third Reich, and who became a representative of the Führer which brought him to the top of the oldest fighting troop of the Party. This position means a lot of appreciation and confidence, as a Stabschef is supposed to train the most valuable young people of the Nation by giving them ideological and physical education and development. For this reason it is confidence and responsibility above all which highlight the task which Stabschef Viktor Lutze performs in the national community.

In the Stabschef's work area in the building of the SA High Command. Berlin is the permanent residence of the Stabschef. However, repeatedly he comes to München to discuss important fundamental questions with the Stabsführer of the SA High Command, SA Obergruppenführer Herzog, in order to make a decision. In mutual agreement the Stabschef and his permanent deputy set the rules for the work and the involvement of the SA.

The Stabsführer of the SA High Command

The Stabsführer, SA Obergruppenführer Herzog, is the permanent deputy of the Stabschef. This position entitles him to authority in all main positions of the SA High Command and the SA Gruppen. His position requires an extraordinary amount of responsibility, the ability to make decisions, and to work. All decisions of a fundamental nature for the SA are not made by the Stabschef, but are made by the Stabsführer. He directly controls the Liaison Office of the SA High Command, the Central Department, the Staff Commandership, the Press and Propaganda Department, the Legal Department and the Architecture Department. Among those the Liaison Office is always in touch with all the important services of the Party and the State to handle any questions which might be of importance for the SA. The Central Department, with its two main departments, takes care of the processing of procedures of a general nature which require the promptest execution and at the same time involve the areas of various main offices which, of course, requires a very good communication with these main offices. The Staff Commandership is responsible for the overall internal services of the SA High Command. The overall press and propaganda preparations and evaluations of all important events within the SA will be performed by the Press and Propaganda Department, which also issues the combat newspaper of the SA High Command, the so-called "SA Mann". The Department has connections to all stations of radio, of films, and also all services within the range of the work scope. According to standards issued by those services, the Gruppe press assistants of the individual SA Gruppen perform their daily tasks and also service the local press. Their activities are mainly to provide information. However, the SA puts no emphasis on the quantitative nature of the paperwork issued about them. On the other hand, we are interested in the German Staff Editor being familiar with their ways and their tasks.

Further, the Department is responsible for the issuance of written paperwork about the SA. The Legal Department is still under construction. However, the Architecture Department, which is also new, is working on the planning and progressing of new SA construction projects which express the SA's new construction willingness, such as new training grounds, SA schools and stadiums.

Could they be speaking concerning the question of the SA Führer recruits? On the wintery snow-covered ground of the SA High Command sports arena at Grünwald close to München, we can see the Stabschef with the Stabsführer in conversation. Just a few minutes ago they had checked out the training site of the SA Führer recruits, so we can assume that this essential question is the subject of their conversation.

The Leadership Headquarters

Chief of the headquarters of the SA High Command is Obergruppenführer Max Jüttner. He is well known to the public and for years the Führer has assigned him leader of the great roll call of all NSDAP organizations on the occasion of the Reicihsparteitag at the Luitpoldhain. In addition, he has to report to the Stabschef concerning the overall organization and structure of the SA, for the education and efficient equipping of the units, and last but not least, for the involvement of the SA.

The headquarters are divided into departments, organizations and actions headed by Brigadeführer Nibbe, and the Department of Physical Exercises under Brigadeführer Michaelis.

The latter is based on the SA Sports Badge to physically train all Germans fit to serve and as preparation for it, to perform physical exercises (physical basic training), to organize the efficiency sports in a way that motivates and attracts people of all levels up to advanced age physically, but also

SA Obergruppenführer Jüttner, as millions of people know him. Early Sunday mornings during the Reichs Party Days they leave for the Luitpold Arena where the Obergruppenführer directs the marching of the SA and the other organizations. Spotlights brighten the twilight and speakers make the commands heard over the whole area. Hour by hour passes as the gigantic, impeccable blocks of the SA, SS, NSKK and the NSFK stand until the great moment when the Führer arrives.

The Chief of the Leadership Headquarters with his closest staff.
Attentively the head of the Office of Physical Exercises, Brigadeführer Michaelis, Obergruppenführer Jüttner, and his Adjutant, Sturmbannführer Berenbock, are looking over the march plan while Brigadeführer Nibbe, who is head of the Organization and Action Office, is speaking. This so-called "paper war" is an indispensable requirement for the success of all those marches which are performed on a large scale.

morally and ideologically.

The output of the Organization and Action Office created its name. Further, it has to service the special SA units, the Communications, Engineer, Naval and Equestrian units, and also the Air and Gas Protection Services of the SA. Other services are the SA Education, the areas of catastrophe protection and prevention of damages, as well as communicating with any other Party and State services related to those.

In addition, the processing of the clothing and equipment of the SA in accordance with the Administrative Main Office, the controlling of the Planning Office by the SA Services Office, as well as the processing of proposals for awarding the so-called "Standartes" and the names of heroic fighters of the Movement to certain SA units.

Again and again the head of the Main Office for Education, SA Obergruppenführer Luyken, and his office chief review the practical results of his work. By clearly following ways that were realized as correct , the Main Office for Education performs its tasks. Constant and active communication with the SA Führers of the front, the cooperation with equal offices of other sections and State organizations guarantee the observance of one uniform way, which also serves the involvement of the SA Führers in task forces. Already today you can see the fruit of these efforts, which will accumulate even more in the years to come.

The Main Office For Education

The Main Office For Education, headed by SA Obergruppenführer Luyken, is responsible for the overall education, training and organization of the SA Führerkorps. Seminars and work groups at the SA Führer Schools of the Reich at Dresden and Münich, as well as at the 21 Gruppe schools and other special schools, serve this purpose. Directly reporting to the Main Office is the Department of Evaluation, headed by Oberführer Girgensohn, which communicates with the Party and the State, and for which, considering the educational work of the SA, the experiences gained by the educational work of the SA produces harmony with the work performed by the Party and all its subdivisions.

The Officer Leadership School of the Reich, headed by Brigadeführer Dame, services the Leadership School of the Reich of the SA in Münich and the Leadership School of the SA High Command in Dresden, out of which the best will be recognized later on. The relatively young Leadership School of the SA High Command in Dresden serves, above all, the education of the middle SA Führerkorps which oversees the qualification to attend one of the Gruppe schools. At present, emphasis is put on the education of the examiners for the SA Sports Badge. The goal of the intellectual and physical education, based on the National Socialistic view, is to make the SA Führers true educators of the team in all fields. Consequently, we will be fully prepared for the major task to form a new German man, filled by the spirit of a political soldier. The triad of soul, spirit and body which, secondarily, unites skills, knowledge and efficiency, is a necessary condition. Military sports, considered by the SA to be physical exercise, is a tool for the education concerning the history of the Party and the Nation, racial studies or the training to become a speaker. The guidelines of this education also apply to the Gruppe schools, headed by Brigadeführer Ivers, although naturally the restriction to the lower SA Führerkorps is expressed in the approved plan. The management of these schools have an SA Führer who has already led a Standarte and who is provided for use in higher services. The work will be delegated, in agreement with the Gruppenführer in whose area the school is located, so that he has the best opportunity to select his junior staff leaders.

The third office, Ideology and Culture, presently headed by SA Obergruppenführer Luyken himself, serves among other things the cultural development, the administration, and cultivation of SA songs, popular songs and folk music. Here it is strictly avoided to issue a schedule for moderate SA ceremonies. It is not the form that is the most important, but the spirit which fulfills the form.

Finally, the Department of Scientific Evaluation, which is under construction, has a voluminous library. Its purpose is to serve and inform each SA Führer who is interested in learning on his own about the most essential existing literature in this area.

The Main Office For Health

The Main Office For Health, headed by Obergruppenführer Brauneck, is responsible for all questions of health and medical services in the SA. As health is the basis and prerequisite for physical exercises, the Main Office For Health is especially involved in this branch of the SA. To the performance of the health service not only belongs the care of the ill and injured, but above all, preventive care. During the time of struggle, we only had the medical service, which today is still especially organized and active. Ten thousand medical men and thousands of medical leaders are well-trained to always be able to give first aid. The SA Medical School of the Reich in Tübingen is the base for the overall training operation in the field of medicine. All Standartes in the whole Reich have medical units available who are ready to step in immediately in case of catastrophes and major severe accidents. The men from the medical service go with their comrades everywhere in the SA service, no matter if it is to public events, cordoning off pack-marches, or sports stadiums. A huge organizational apparatus runs through the entire SA and carries the symbol of the life rune as the symbol of the fight for maintaining health. Schooling, equipment and organization of the medical services are consolidated into the Main Office For Health, and next to it stands the second office for health leadership with the tasks for racial care. As with all decisive questions in the life of the Nation and in the field of public health, the best propaganda are those tough and experienced fighters for public health for the new German men, the SA men. We have realized the value of the health of the Nation and are convinced that only a healthy nation will be a permanent nation. We convincingly fight for the guidelines and instructions issued by the Headquarters Office for Public Health and by the Reichs Medical Führer. In the front line stands the medical men of the SA who make themselves one for the great goal, purity of the blood and purity of the race.

Not curing, but maintaining.
The Chief of the Main Office for Public Healthcare, SA Obergruppenführer Brauneck, considers his most important task to be preventive care.
The repeated inspections of the medical facilities of the SA also serve it and this aspect also plays an important role when educating the SA medical leaders and the men. The doctor not only cares for the body, but also for the soul. The SA medical men unselfishly serve the community, but they are also propagandists for the purity of blood and race of the people.

To involve the right men at the right place.

At the front, in the staffs, and the SA schools, the knowledge and skills of the SA Führers all come into effect. Evaluation of the results received will be performed by the Personnel Headquarters, whose head is SA Gruppenführer Raeke (sitting), here in a conversation with SA Brigadeführer Damian (middle), who is leader of the courts and legal offices, and SA Brigadeführer Bock, head of the Office of Social Welfare. The personnel data of all higher and full-time middle SA Führers have been registered by the headquarters, which makes decisions about their evaluation and efficiency.

The Personnel Main Office

The SA received a challenging educational task from the Führer, in which the whole German Nation is included in the execution. As now each SA Mann is supposed to be an example for his comrades, this applies to the SA Führer at a higher level. The care for the SA Führerkorps, as well as for the SA Führer recruits, therefore is a problem which not only is of major importance for their positions, but also for the Party and the whole Nation.

The Personnel Main Office, whose head is SA Gruppenführer Raeke, is divided into three sub-offices: Personnel (Brigadeführer Boetel), Social Welfare, and the Legal Office, and constantly communicates with the SA front where the spirit and suitability of the SA Führers are shown on a daily basis. Frequent changes between the front, the work of the staff, and being used for educational purposes, mark the SA Führer's career. Evaluation is done considering moral suitability, spirit and knowledge, but above all, his service for the Movement. The oldest marchers and fighters in the SA also take leading positions within the divisions, if talented. A review of all of the personnel files of all higher and middle-level SA Führers who are registered by these authorities shows that the SA shortly will be in a position to supply the men to the Party who will be necessary to salvage the German Nation.

Even if appreciation for the older fighters partly is

a bigger responsibility, the Office of Social Care makes sure that those SA comrades will be taken care of who were injured fighting for the new Germany or who are in the red otherwise. For the first few years after taking over power the main goal was to provide work for the men, but now emphasis is being put on the problem of retraining them. At the camps Lockstedt and Falkenstein the SA gives the opportunity to unskilled people to acquire the journeyman certification in approximately 40 weeks, which improves their qualifications to find industrial employment as a skilled worker in those branches with under-employment. Furthermore, men are being retrained for commercial jobs and to work in the administration services. However, the SA not only appreciates the requirements of the old fighters, but also serves the goals of the four-year plan in an excellent way.

The same applies to the selection of settlers for those homes arising out of the fund of the Nation's "Thanks Offerings" all over the Reich. Also here, in addition to the war sacrifices, the old fighters are the ones looking for a new home in the "Thanks Offering" housing areas.

In addition to the professional care, there is the personal care of the men and their families who suffered injuries during physical exercises or on the job. They will receive a paid vacation to go to a spa or rehabilitation center, such as SA-Home Wyk on Föhr, Hohenlychen, or Trillup near Hamburg. If necessary, they will be supported by agreement of the Treasurer of the Reich, by funds out of the Adolf Hitler Dank and out of the Adolf Hitler Spende.

Above all, the office headed by Chief SA Brigadeführer Bock takes care of those who were wounded by political opponents in the time of struggle by making sure to these men that their sacrifices will never be forgotten.

The third within the Personnel Headquarters is the Legal Office, headed by SA Brigadeführer Damian. The main function of this office is to give awards, and the purity maintenance of the SA and of the SA Führerkorps.

For this purpose there are two disciplinary chambers. A special department handles the personal rights of the SA man.

The Legal Department, staffed by special attorneys, deals with other tasks such as legal advice to the Headquarters of the SA High Command and the Gruppen, the communication with other legal authorities of the Movement, and third, communication with the office of the Führer, as well as the processing of petitions for review of convicted SA men and ex-SA members, considering that the SA man on one hand has an increased responsibility to the national community, and on the other hand, with respect to old proven SA fighters, frequently economical and mental consequences from the time of the struggle for power were present which can only be judged fully by the SA. Especially the old comrade has a right to have his SA comrades on his side when he considers himself threatened concerning legal affairs. However, this obligation of the SA is met as far as possible considering the situation.

The Administration Main Office

The SA administration in its present standard organization and clean housekeeping represents the tool which the Stabschef requires to handle the tasks he receives from the Führer. Clarity is the symbol of the SA administration in all its areas.

Per the Unitary Law of December 1, 1933 and its rules, the financial and legal affairs of the NSDAP and the SA are controlled by the Treasurer of the Reich, who is authorized by the Führer. The Treasurer of the Reich authorizes the Treasure Administrator, SA Gruppenführer Mappes, for the overall SA administration who, in addition to his responsibility to the Treasurer of the Reich, at the same time is the head of the Main Administration Office and the Stabschef's deputy for all administrative affairs of the total SA.

The scope of the Administrative Main Office is divided into three offices: (a)Finances, Housekeeping, Accounting, Financial, and Economic Control; (b)Materials, Purchases, Insurance and Contracts; and (c)Construction and Relocation Office. The pay for all full-time SA Führers and their men is controlled by the authorities. It consists of basic salaries, housing, child and spouse support. Child support is especially regulated in socially excellent rates which is due to the popular political view.

Greatest thrift is a matter of course, especially in the SA, and is always mentioned on every occasion. The well-working payroll and control system gives exact figures concerning the economical housekeeping of all units, and facilitates and takes immediate action concerning possible deficiencies. The control reports are the responsibility of the

Here you see one of the "Thanks Offering" housing areas shortly before its completion.
In all areas of the Reich, the Chief of the Administrative Main Office, Grüppenführer Mappes, together with his deputy over all of the SA settlements, Sturmbahnführer Konwiarz, check on the status of the work in those settlements, which were built by funds out of the "Thanks Offering of the Nation". The result of this socialistic action is happy and satisfied people in their own homes, and even here in Gräfelsing close to Münich beaming faces say thank you to the responsible men of the SA.

Correctness and neatness are Rule No. 1 in the SA.
Gruppenführer Mappes also created, among other things, a special book-keeping for the SA which enables a quick and efficient control of all asset values and their usage up to the Stürmes. Further, the SA pay order is exemplary, either socially speaking or considering the popular, political education work. All measures required are performed in true SA-like spirit.

Treasurer of the Reich in all units and are posted and evaluated in a special department of the Administration Headquarters.

The great assets of the SA, which are part of the total assets of the NSDAP, are registered by quantity and value and carefully administered. On this occasion may be mentioned the meaning of the SA to the German economy, which just by the completion of rent, lease and insurance contracts, as well as repairs, makes an annual present of several million Reichsmarks. In addition to acquiring motor vehicles and accessories, the SA men themselves spend many millions for their clothing and equipment per year.

Many millions go to the economy due to the settlement project created by the SA High Command, supported by the so-called "Thanks Offering of the Nation", by which 3,000 needy and multiple-child families are supposed to get their own home. In addition to suburb housing areas, the Construction and Relocation Office built farm settlements with 60 to 80 acres of land close to Aurich, which overall are worked by ex-farm workers. Also here livestock and even harvesting are supplied free.

The remarkable tasks of the SA Administration are totally related to the growth of the leadership. Marches and other events, schooling, equipment, purchases, etc. cannot be performed without the cooperation of the Administration.

Reporting to the Stabschef.
Daily the Chief of the Adjutantcy,
Gruppenführer Reimann, reports to the
Stabschef in order to make decisions concern-
ing important questions.

The Adjutantcy

In Berlin at the Vosstrasse, which is adjacent to the Reichs Chancellory, is the simple and plain Prussian construction in which the Adjutantcy of the Stabschef resides. Here at the Adjutantcy, headed by Gruppenführer Reimann, who also is head of the Standarte "Feldherrnhalle", all questions are processed which come from duty stations of the Party and the State, as well as others. Every day the Adjutant gets a stack of mail, and has to sort the letters according to their importance and to report to the Stabschef concerning the most important affairs. Many letters express confidence in the SA men, and even if a major part of them deals with things which could as well be handled by the responsible unit leaders, it means they were sent to the Adjutantcy by skipping the regular way. They try their best to resolve the most essential cases, if possible.

In addition to those tasks, the responsible men in the Adjutantcy have to make sure that the journeys of the Stabschef are well prepared and made without any trouble. Again and again the Stabschef visits the individual Gruppen, mainly by plane, but also by train and car. All the detail

work required by these business trips requires prompt execution for meeting deadlines and performing the whole program as planned. The two Adjutants of the Stabschef, Brigadeführer Heitmüller and Obersturmbahnführer Hermel, who at the same time is the Chief of the Culture Circle of the SA, take turns in accompanying the Stabschef on each of his trips and therefore are witnesses to the love and affection he receives again and again. Even in visiting the individual Gruppen and their marches, Führer roll calls and the sports tournaments, they always show the same picture to the spectator; however, each individual event would be an unforgettable experience for the men, who as companions of the Stabschef, see the eternal spirit of the Sturmabteilung in the columns of political soldiers from all areas of the Reich. The same applies to the simple fighter wearing the brown shirt to whom the Stabschef's words are directed as a source of power concerning the ideological composition of the political daily life. Naturally, many SA Führers who happen to be in the capitol of the Reich come to the Adjutantcy in person to talk to the Stabschef. Many miscellaneous matters are presented and some valuable suggestions come from the visitors. If it even needs to be mentioned, most of the matters could have been handled by the Standartes or Gruppen as well. However, the men whose task it is to personally serve the Stabschef, answer at least the most important questions or refer the comrades to the duty station which is responsible for the matter in question. Additionally, the miscellaneous business meetings of the Stabschef with the leading men in the Party and State has to be scheduled and the agenda has to be set according to the requirements so that all works and tasks can be performed without any delay. The men in the Adjutantcy do not have an easy life, but knowing that they help their comrades everywhere in the Reich and that they support their fight is sufficient appreciation to them.

Work conference at the Adjutantcy.
On a regular basis, the heads of the departments meet with the Chief of the Adjutantcy in order to set the guidelines for their department works. From left to right: Standartenführer Besserer, Gruppenführer Reimann, Obersturmbannführer Hermel (Chief of the Culture Circle and 2nd Adjutant), Brigadeführer Heitmüller (1st Adjutant) and Standartenführer Dill (Administration).

By the way, the systematic training in horseback riding according to Army guidelines shows that the horses used were not senselessly used but, on the contrary, were also trained and therefore their value increased.

At the same time, considering the development of figures, the training value of the NSRK was increased. On the occasion of 1,056 official riding exams given in 1937, 22,413 rider certificates were issued.

Due to the Führer and Chancellor of the Reich, the National Socialist Rider Korps (NSRK) was set up in the spring of 1936 and put under the Inspector for Riding and Driving Training of the Reich, SA Obergruppenführer Litzmann (middle), who directly reports to the Stabschef.

*

Picture to the left:

The Main Office of the NS Sports Competitions.

On November 27, 1936 the Führer released the following decree: "Following my proclamation on the occasion of the Reichs Party Day of Honor I herewith create the National Socialistic Sports Competitions for all future Reichs Party Days. The SA will manage these competitions concerning the preparation and performance. The necessary instructions will be issued according to the suggestions of the SA Stabschef. The Sports Führer of the Reich will be assigned Sports Referee and will cooperate with the SA High Command. The Stabschef will regularly inform me about the planned measures."

In order to resolve all tasks organizationally in accordance with the Führer's decree, the Main Office of Competitions of the SA High Command was created in February, 1937. Sports Führer of the Reich, von Tschammer und Osten, had been assigned Chief of the Main Office of Sports Competitions by the Stabschef. This assignment guaranteed the close cooperation with the Reich, a union for physical training to resolve the tasks imposed by the Führer concerning military training of the whole Nation and the creation of a Nation by physical exercises. SA Obergruppenführer von Tschammer und Osten is responsible for the organization and performance of the annual NS Sports Competitions which take place at the Reichs Party Days at Nuremberg, and specifically presentation of the performance awards for the whole German Nation. At the same time the Main Office is supposed to organize and manage the NS winter games, which also increase continuously, and annually take place at well-known German winter sports centers. The Main Office for SA Games is divided into three sections: Organization, Military Sports and Sports. Its main office is in Berlin, at W8, Unter den Linden 53.

Picture to the right:

The National Socialist Rider Korps.

The development of the National Socialist Rider Korps (NSRK) shows that its function was necessary and its organization right. Finally the threatening disintegration of riding was stopped and an organization was created in which, according to the requirements and standards of the Army, a general and equal basic training in horseback riding and driving can be passed. Thousands of breeders guarantee the solidarity of the NSRK with the German peasantry. They realize that the basic conditions for breeding are promotion of love for horses, the joy of sports, and the wish to join the Army in order to serve the Nation. The NSRK nowadays has almost 100,000 riders, out of whom more than 80,000 are farmers or farmer's sons.

For training the NSRK has more than 80,000 horses available. This sacrifice, which was unselfishly made by the individual horse owners, was acknowledged by the Führer and Chancellor of the Reich by the foundation of the Badge of Appreciation.

THE GRUPPENFÜHRERS OF THE SA

Right: Gruppenführer Richard Wagenbauer.
Gruppenführer Richard Wagenbauer was born at Germersheim, Rheinpfalz on June 30, 1896. He attended elementary school, classical high school and six classes of the Royal Bavarian Cadet School and qualified for college.

Gruppenführer Wagenbauer served in the 1st and 2nd Bavarian Foot Artillery Regiment and in various area departments from August, 1914 through June, 1918. His last rank was Oberleutnant. He is carrier of the EK I and EK. II, as well as the Wound Badge in black, the War Honor Cross and the BMVD, 4th class with swords.

In 1919 Gruppenführer Wagenbauer was a member of the Freikorps Epp, as well as of the Hierl and Probstmayer detachment; 1924-28 he was a member of the Front Fighter Union. Since October 1, 1930, Gruppenführer Wagenbauer has been a member of the Party (member number 502,919). October 1, 1930 he joined the SS and on October 1, 1932 he joined the SA. Since May 15, 1937, he has been Führer of the Gruppe Bavarian Ostmark.

Left: Obergruppenführer von Jagow.
Führer of the Gruppe Berlin-Brandenburg.
Born February 29, 1892 at Frankfurt (Oder) he attended college to become an officer. From 1912-20, Obergruppenführer von Jagow was an active Naval officer. During the war he was an officer on duty on SM U-boat UB 77. Holder of the EK. I and II and U-boat War Badge. In 1920 Obergruppenführer von Jagow resigned. After the war he experienced the fights of the Second Naval Brigade and the border patrol Oberschlesischen in 1921. For many years he was Führer of the SA Württemberg. His first joining of the Movement was in 1920; his second joining of the Party and SA was on January 1, 1929. In 1931 he was Führer of the Gruppe Südwest. During the National Revolt, he was Commissar of the Reich for Wurttemberg. On July 20, 1934 he was charged with building the leadership of the Gruppe Berlin-Brandenburg and on September 15, 1935 was assigned Führer of this Gruppe. Obergruppenführer von Jagow is Prussian State Counselor, Province Counselor, Senator of the City of Berlin, member of the People's Court of Law, Kaptain-Leutnant of the Reserve, and member of the Reichstag since May, 1932.

Obergruppenführer von Obernitz.
Obergruppenführer Hans-Günther von Obernitz was born May 5, 1899 at Düsseldorf.
War service as Fahnenjunker senior grade of the Guard Füsilier Regiment, January 25, 1917 until the end of the war. He served at the front as platoon leader, company leader (MGK), administrative and MG officer, and Battalion Adjutant. In September, 1919 he was dismissed from active service. EK. I and EK. II, as well as many other badges. For the first time Obergruppenführer von Obernitz offered his services to the Movement with Ullrich Klintzsch in Münich in 1923 on the occasion of setting up the first SA "Hundertschaften". Since March 25, 1933, Obergruppenführer von Obernitz has been Führer of the Gruppe Franconia. He was promoted to his present rank November 9, 1937.

Obergruppenführer Siegfried Kasche.
Obergruppenführer Siegfried Kasche was born on June 18, 1903 in Strausberg (Ostbahn). He attended the Victoria College Potsdam, Cadet Korps Potsdam and Lichterfelde. After the closing of the Cadet Korps, he joined the Army in October, 1918. He had participated in the fights in Berlin and the Baltic in 1919. In the end he was cadet and company leader in service at the workers' union in Pommern in 1920 and 1921. In his professional life he spent about two years each in agriculture, banking, the glass industry, and textile industry. He was always active in military unions and politics. On January 9, 1926 Obergruppenführer Kasche joined the Party (member number 27,478) and the SA. He has been a member of the Reichstag since the Fifth Election Period in 1930. From January 7, 1932 to March 15, 1934, he was Führer of the Gruppe Ostmark, and from July 12, 1934 to October 31, 1937, Führer of the Gruppe Niedersachsen; since November 1, 1937 Obergruppenführer Kasche has been Führer of the Gruppe Hansa.

Left: Obergruppenführer Adolf Heinz Beckerle.

He was born February 4, 1902 in Frankfurt am Main. Attended classical high school. Easter 1921 he graduated. He studied political economy, law and philosophy; he received a diploma in political economy. He worked several years in industrial, commercial and banking facilities. His business trips took him to North America and South America. Out of these he spent one year in Argentina and Paraguay.

The first time he joined the Party was on August 29, 1922 under member number 7,197; he joined the Party a second time (member number 80,983) and the SA on January 9, 1928. He was a member of the Prussian Legislature during the Fourth Election Period until September, 1932. He has been a member of the Reichstag since the Sixth Election Period in 1932. He has been Police President in Frankfurt am Main, and from January 7, 1933, Führer of the Gruppe Hessen.

Above: Obergruppenführer Wilhelm Helfer.

He was born on December 26, 1886 at Kaiserslautern (Pfalz). He attended grade school and classical high school. Commercial on-the-job training.

War service: Imperial Protection Trupp of German Southwest Africa. Returned to Germany in 1922. Immediately upon return he joined the NSDAP under member number 395.

Obergruppenführer Helfer has been holder of the Blood Order since November 9, 1923. Since the Ninth Election Period in 1933 he has been member of the Reichstag; from July 10, 1934 he has been Führer of the Gruppe Hochland.

Gruppenführer Herbert Fust.

He was born at Langenfelde (Pommern) on June 1, 1899. He attended grade school at Glewitz in Demmin, college at Demmin, school for agriculture at Eldena (Pommern), and after passing the final exams joined the one-year volunteer service. After the final exams, he voluntarily joined the Army and was dismissed in May, 1919. Since then he has been working as a farmer.

Gruppenführer Fust joined the Party and the SA on November 15, 1930. From September 15, 1933 through October 31, 1937, he was Führer of the Gruppe Hansa. He has been a member of the Reichstag since the Eighth Election Period in 1933. From November 1, 1937 he has been Führer of the Gruppe Kurpfalz.

Obergruppenführer Adolf Kob.

He was born in Prague on June 7, 1885. He attended grade school and college at Dresden and München. In 1906 he became an officer in the 6th Royal Sachsischen Field Artillery Regiment 68 at Riesa. In 1912 he attended the War Academy in Berlin. During the war he was Division Adjutant and later General Staff Officer, as well as Commander of the 3rd Division of the Field Artillery Regiment 68. After the war he said goodbye and became a Police officer for the Sachsischen District Police. In 1923 the socialist, communist government Zeigner terminated him. From then on he worked for an industrial enterprise.

Obergruppenführer Kob has been in the Movement since February 1, 1930. First he had various SA positions in the Gruppe Sachsen. In 1933 he was a member of the Sachsen legislature, and has been a member of the Reichstag since the Ninth Election Period in 1933. From September 15, 1933 through January 31, 1934, he was Führer of the Gruppe Ostland. From February 1, 1934 through July 9, 1934, Inspector East. From July 10, 1934 he has been Führer of the Gruppe Mitte.

THE GRUPPENFÜHRERS OF THE SA

Obergruppenführer Heinrich Knickmann.
He was born at Horstermark on September 25, 1894. He attended grade school, college and officer's training school. During the war he was wounded twice. As an officer, he received the EK. II and miscellaneous other badges. After the war he became a member of self-protection and border protection unions. After his training at the communal administration service he found employment with the administration of the City of Buer. In 1923 he became the leader of the active defense war against the French-Belgian Army in the area of Emscher-Lippe. From 1924 he was Organization Officer at the Korps Area Headquarters VI at Munster, Westfalen.
Obergruppenführer Knickmann had already joined the NSDAP on December 15, 1922. At the same time he also joined the SA. During the prohibition era, Obergruppenführer Knickmann was a member of the SA Prohibition "Union of Old Comrades". On March 10, 1925, after re-foundation of the Party, he joined it a second time (member number 16,106). Obergruppenführer Knickmann is holder of the Golden Party Badge. He was a member of the Reichstag. Since July 1, 1933 he has been Führer of the Gruppe Niederrhein.

The "Gruppe" is the largest SA unit and its leadership accordingly issues tasks which bring an extraordinary degree of responsibility with them, as well as the requirements of willingness to act and to work. The Gruppe Führers of the SA again and again showed their talent during the long and tough years of fighting. They are all Adolf Hitler's oldest and most efficient co-fighters who, at the front of a small crowd of political soldiers of the Führer at that time, made way for the National Socialist ideology to the German people's hearts. The leader personality is not proven at the green table, but at the front. While the so-called Marxist "leaders", as well as the organizations of the political Catholicism, are not meant to be seen in the assaults they had planned, while these noblemen only were great when they could speak big words without threatening their own persons, SA Führers were always there at the head of their men, no matter if it was protection at meetings or propaganda marches. The leaders always had to be good examples and they were. Not just from the feeling of being comrades and the consciousness that the team could rely on the Führer as well as he could rely on his men, this SA fighting union was built which could pass even the hardest tests. Even today the leaders of the SA still work and fight according to this spirit.

A Gruppenführer's personality is essential and directed toward attendance and the spirit of the men within the Gruppe he is heading. He coordinates the involvement and tasks according to the guidelines and standards issued by the Stabschef, as well as the cooperation of the Party's divisions

Obergruppenführer Arthur Bockenhauer.
He was born on September 13, 1899 at Hamburg. Commercial on-the-job training. Before and during the war he was active in the militaristic youth preparation and voluntarily joined the Army. He served at the Western Front and received the Badge. Wounded once. After the war he continued serving in the Army (Freikorps, temporary Reichswehr, and the Reichswehr) and in 1923 was a bank employee. 1920-22 he was active in various popular organizations. He has been a member of the NSDAP since 1922. SA Führer at Hamburg since early 1923. After the prohibition of the Party, he illegally continued to lead the SA Hamburg as "Domestic, Sports and Walking Union Blucher of 1923" until 1925. From 1925 he was SA Führer in Hamburg again on the re-foundation of the Party. On November 2, 1926 the Hamburg Police Department dismissed him without notice due to his NSDAP activities. On September 27, 1931 and April 24, 1932 they made him a member of the Hamburg Citizens. In 1933 he was Führer of the Gruppe Hansa, Hamburg. Since March 1, 1934 he has served on the Staff of the SA High Command and from April 1, 1935 he was Office Chief of the Courts and Legal Office of the SA High Command until October 31, 1937. From November 1, 1937, he has been Führer of the Gruppe Niedersachsen. Member of the Reichstag.

Obergruppenführer Joachim Meyer-Quade.
He was born on November 22, 1897 at Düsseldorf. He attended high school for one year. On January 21, 1915 he voluntarily joined the Field Artillery Regiment 84, and on November 1, 1915 he joined the Infantry Regiment 99 at Flandern, Verdun, Somme, and was in French captivity. After the sixth attempt to escape, he got out on January 2, 1920. EK II and EK I. Farm activities and agricultural press from 1920 through 1930. Member of the Reichstag since 1930.
He joined the Party on June 13, 1925 (member number 7,608), and the SA on July 1, 1927. Obergruppenführer Meyer-Quade is holder of the Golden Party Badge. Since February 1, 1934 he has been Führer of the Gruppe Nordmark, and since May, 1934, Police President at Kiel.

Gruppenführer Heinrich Böhmcker
He was born on July 22, 1896 at Braak (Gutin). He attended elementary school at Braak, college at Gutin, University at Kiel, Gottingen and Munster and studied law at the Courts. In 1927, he was Assessor of Exams and a lawyer in Gutin. In 1932, he was Government President of Oldenburg.
Gruppenführer Böhmcker was in the service from August 9, 1914, served in the 3rd Reserve Squadron and Dragoon Regiment 16, Lüneburg and Cavalry Division 78, as well as 8 Battery of the First Guard Foot Artillery Regiment.
Gruppenführer Böhmcker joined the Party on January 11, 1926 (member number 27,601), after already having joined the SA on December 26, 1925. He is holder of the Golden Party Badge. Since April 16, 1937, Gruppenführer Böhmcker has been Mayor of the Free City of Bremen and from July 10, 1934, Führer of the Gruppe Nordsee.

and the State within his field. The public knows most of these leaders. It knows that they are sitting with their men at the camps and on the occasion of sports activities as comrade among comrades. It also knows that in the SA this good relationship between leadership and the front plays an important part in the exemplary spirit of this structure, which will be expressed on the occasion of each involvement concerning service in the community. The Gruppenführer is not more valuable than his men, but he has the first burden

of an increased responsibility to the Stabschef and the Supreme SA Führer, Adolf Hitler.

The SA is a union of fighters and at the head of such a union can only be men who do not know fighting from books, but from experience. You will notice that following the development of the SA Gruppenführers, they have actively participated in all of the events which were unforgettable milestones on the way to the new Reich. We saw them as the hub of the red Berlin East with its violent hall fights. They were standing in front

Below: Obergruppenführer Arno Manthey.

He was born on September 6, 1888 at Schubin (Posen). He attended elementary school in Schubin, and secondary school in Bromberg until Prima. He studied agriculture and became a farmer on his own farm.

He was a war volunteer, wounded three times. As an officer he received the EK I, EK II and various other badges. In January, 1919 he organized the German resistance against the Polish revolt at the District Retze, Schubin-Bromberg. He was a representative for the Province Brandenburg.

On October 1, 1930 Obergruppenführer Manthey joined the Party and the SA. Since July 10, 1934 he has been Führer of the Gruppe Ostmark. He has been a member of the Reichstag since the Ninth Election Period in 1933.

Obergruppenführer Heinrich Schoene.

He was born on November 25, 1889 in Berlin. He attended Bismarck College at Berlin-Wilmersdorf, then agricultural school at Dahme (Mark) and passed the finals as a senior. He worked as a farmer and agricultural officer.

He did service in Infantry Regiment 140 from August 2, 1914 through November, 1918. He was wounded twice.

Since August 14, 1925 he has been a member of the NSDAP (member number 17,091), and since April 20, 1925, a member of the SA. From February 15, 1932 through January 31, 1934, he was Führer of the Gruppe Nordmark, and from February 1, 1934, Führer of the Gruppe Ostland. Police President at Königsberg, District Gruppenführer of the Civil Air Defense in Eastern Prussia, member of the District Council and Rural Farmers Council, Eastern Prussia, and on the Chamber of Employment, Eastern Prussia. He was a member of the Prussian Legislature 1932-33 and of the Reichstag since the Ninth Election Period in 1933.

with their men in Hamburg when the Marxists were being pushed back step by step under considerable sacrifices. Thousands of small, unknown SA men were in position at the coal mines and their posts when they learned of the familiar gray specter of unemployment. These are the men who nowadays are heading the SA Gruppes which were formed by their spirits.

Below: Obergruppenführer Wilhelm Schepmann.

He was born on June 17, 1894 in Hattingen (Ruhr). He attended elementary school, college, prep school and teacher's seminar.

War service: November 9, 1914 through January 22, 1915, training at Jäger 7; from January 23, 1915, platoon leader at the western and eastern war fronts; Company Führer, Battalion Adjutant, wounded severely.

Obergruppenführer Schepmann joined the Movement for the first time in 1923. After re-foundation of the Party, on December 28, 1925, he joined a second time. At the same time he also joined the SA. Obergruppenführer Schepmann is holder of the Golden Party Badge (member number 26,762). From February 17, 1933 through November 14, 1934, he was Police President at Dortmund. Member of the Prussian Legislature from 1932 through 1933; Reichstag member since the Ninth Election Period in 1933. District Hauptmann at Dresden-Bautzen, and from July 16, 1934, he has been Führer of the Gruppe Sachsen.

Obergruppenführer Heinrich Bennecke.

He was born February 8, 1902 in Dresden. He attended elementary school, classical high school (baccalaureate), studied at the Technical College at Dresden, University at München and Leipzig (June 10, 1930 – Doctorate in Philosophy at Leipzig), then staff editor.

In 1921 he served in the Freikorps Hassfurther at Oberschlesien. In 1922, Obergruppenführer Bennecke joined the Movement for the first time. On May 15, 1925, after the re-foundation of the Party, he joined the second time (member number 4,840). Obergruppenführer Bennecke is holder of the Blood Order of November 9, 1923, the Coburg Badge and the Golden Party Badge. He was a member of the Sachsischen Legislature from June, 1930 through October, 1933. From 1934 until the end of 1936, Obergruppenführer Bennecke has been Führer of the Gruppe Pommern.

Gruppenführer Heinrich George Graf Finck von Finckenstein.

He was born on November 22, 1894. He received his schooling at home (home teacher), Humanistic College at Greifenberg to upper secondary.

August 2, 1914 at the Dragoon Regiment Bredow, Schlesisches No. 4 in Lüben. On November 1, 1914 in the field with the active regiment. On February 15, 1915, he was promoted to Leutnant. May, 1917, Führer of signals unit. EK I and EK II, as well as other badges. Last rank: Oberleutnant. After the war he joined the Freikorps.

Gruppenführer Graf Finck von Finckenstein joined the NSDAP for the first time in 1923. After re-foundation of the Party, he joined a second time on September 25, 1925 (member number 19,599). He is holder of the Golden Party Badge. Since August 15, 1936, he has been Führer of the Gruppe Schlesien.

Obergruppenführer Hanns Lubin.

He was born June 10, 1905 in Freiburg (Breisgau). He attended elementary school, Humanistic College (baccalaureate), Infantry School (cadet exams), Artillery School (officer's exams), and five semesters at University at Tubingen. From 1924 through 1930, German Army (artillery officer). In Spring, 1930 Obergruppenführer Lubin received one and one-half years in prison for what they called National Socialistic cell formation. Then Führer of the SA Second Gruppe Baden. He joined the Party on October 1, 1930. From March through April, 1935 he was Deputy Police President at Karlsruhe. He has been a member of the Reichstag since the Sixth Election Period in 1932. From April, 1933 he has been Führer of the Gruppe Südwest.

Gruppenführer Kurt Günther.

He was born on October 31, 1896 in Gera. 1903 through 1912 he attended high school at Gera. Through 1915 technical surveying and cultural engineering and training to do service. 1915 through 1918 he was a war participant. Front service in the East and West in Mine Laying Company 408. In 1918, after being trained by the Royal Prussian Land Registration in Berlin and the Technical University at Stuttgart, he was a topographer and trigonometer at Survey Department 8 (Vogesen).

In 1922 he joined the NSDAP for the first time at Hirschberg Saale. On February 15, 1926 he joined the Party (member number 30,179) and the SA a second time. Gruppenführer Günther is holder of the Golden Party Badge. Since March 1, 1935 he has been Führer of the Gruppe Thuringen. Since February 27,

1936 he has been Counselor of State in the Land Service of Thuringia. He is also a member of the Chamber of Employment in middle Germany. He was a member of the Reichstag during the Sixth Election Period in 1932 and since the Eighth Election Period in 1933.

Obergruppenführer Otto Schramme.

He was born on October 1, 1898 in Berlin. First he attended the Community School, then junior high school and Kirchner High School in Berlin. He was a civil recruit for the government in Potsdam, then head accountant at the Financial Administration of the RFV Reich. War participant from 1917 through 1919, wounded severely. Unteroffizier and officer candidate. EK II and Front Fighter Honor Badge. In 1920 he was an officer at the RFV Financial Administration of the Reich and in the end the Chief Tax Inspector.

Obergruppenführer Schramme has been a member of the NSDAP since early 1924 (member number 28,705), and since July 1, 1925 he has been a member of the SA. From 1932 to 1933 he was a member of the Prussian Legislature, and member of the Reichstag since the Ninth Election Period in 1933. Since December 11, 1934, Police President at Dortmund. Since July 10, 1934, he has been Führer of the Gruppe Westfalen.

Gruppenführer Günther Gräntz.

He was born on July 26, 1905 in Frankfurt am Main. He attended high school and college (baccalaureate). Political and legal studies at Universities Frankfurt am Main and Münich.

Gruppenführer Gräntz joined the Party (member number 5,274) and the SA in 1925. From March through November, 1933, he was a member of the Prussian Legislature, at the same time he was also a member of the Kommunal Legislature at Wiesbaden and a member of the District Legislation at Kassel. From February through April, 1934 he was a civil counselor at Frankfurt am Main. Gruppenführer Gräntz held various SA ranks and since October 1, 1936 he has been Führer of the Gruppe Westmark.

Obergruppenführer Hermann Reschny.

He was born on June 15, 1898 at Stammersdorf close to Vienna. He attended elementary school and then the teacher's seminar at Feldkirch. He was active in the service from 1916 through 1919 in Russia and Italy. Infantry officer. From 1919 through 1933 he was a teacher in the City of Vienna. In 1932 he served as a member of the Parliament of Lower Austria, and then he was a member of the Austrian Legislature until 1933.

In 1921 Obergruppenführer Reschny joined the File Trupp, which was the SA's pre-curser in Vienna. In 1923 the File Trupp was renamed the SA and in July, 1926 it was integrated into the German SA. Since that time Obergruppenführer Reschny was Führer of the Austrian SA until 1933. On September 15, 1935 he was assigned Führer of the Relief Organization Northwest. He has held that position to the present day.

HERMANN GÖRING

Minister President and SA Obergruppenführer Hermann Göring walks together with the Stabschef to review the march past of the SA Standarte "Felderrnhalle"
On the celebration of his 44th birthday, the first SA Führer receives the appointment document signed by the Führer making him Chief of the Standarte "Feldherrnhalle". By this another link had been created between the SA and Hermann Göring which even more expresses the good relationships of the Minister President with the men of the Sturmabteilung.

So wie die SA. vor der Machtübernahme das Rückgrat der Bewegung war, so wird sie es auch in Zukunft bleiben. Die Art ihres Kampfes hat sich zwar äußerlich geändert, aber nach wie vor hat die SA. die Aufgabe, den Geist unseres Führers im Volke voranzutragen.

SA.-Obergruppenführer

The way the SA was the backbone of the Movement before taking over power, the same way it will be in the future. The method of fighting only changed on the surface. However the SA is still responsible for bringing forward the spirit of our Führer to the people.

SA Obergruppenführer
(signature)
Hermann Göring

When on the Sunday of the SA the endless brown columns are marching in decorated Nuremberg, there also Hermann Göring stands next to Adolf Hitler's car, along with the Stabschef and the former OSAF von Pfeffer, and looks into the eyes of the men wearing the brown shirts whose first leader he once was and who still are proud to call themselves his comrades. On his birthday the year before, he was very pleased to be assigned Chief of the SA Standarte "Feldherrnhalle". As a new sign of his close relationship to the political soldiers of the Führer, solidarity is expressed by the Minister President again and again. It started in those days when Hermann Göring found his way to Adolf Hitler. Erich

With lots of enthusiasm, the SA receives "our Hermann".
The unusual popularity which SA Obergruppenführer Göring has as one of Adolf Hitler's oldest and most efficient fighting comrades, can especially be seen on the occasion of his visit to SA Camp Langwasser during a Party rally. Thousands of hands are being stretched out and each one would like to take an autograph home with him; thus the men in brown shirts consider Hermann Göring to be one of theirs, who they appreciate as leader and comrade.

Gritzbach wrote in his book issued by the Central Party Publisher, "Hermann Göring, Work and Man", the following about it:

"In 1922 Adolf Hitler is speaking. In the crowd listening to his words is the Flight Captain, the last commander of the Richtofen-Geschwader, with his young wife. Still the small crowd is looking at the man who develops his thoughts ideologically, hoping to rouse in the people the sleeping consciousness of the nation with the full power of his personality, who first talks about freedom and honor and then about work and bread. Yes, this is a fanatic; a fanatic to believe in the recreation of the German soul and the German power. This speech is shaped by his creativity as if Hitler already had the responsibility for Germany and its people.

The meeting is filled with a lot of excitement. People are looking at each other in agreement, people who have never met before; however, who know that the words spoken by the man above them will link them to each other. Very excited, Göring is holding his wife's hand, who feels her husband's emotions as can only be felt by a woman. This hour of experience passes like a vision. When both are outside again, Göring is sure that the die of his life is cast."

The next day two men who have been marching side by side for fifteen years shake hands. On this day, the follower gave himself to the Führer. He received a major task and a high goal. Hitler gave Göring the care and training of the Sturmabteilung and the love of his countrymen from that day on. From this hour on the SA Mann and the divisions are awaiting the command to attack from the Führer.

His headquarters are at Obermenzing, but he always stays with the Führer. Deeper and deeper he gets into the thoughts of the man who will form Germany's destiny. With the increase of the Movement the young SA is also growing, as well as the brown battalions. It's a pleasure to be alive! This life has unknown pleasures and a marvelous goal and the task means service as workers and officers, students and farmers, who are molded into one unit. Service and again service. It is not only intellectual training, but also with guns, machine guns and trucks

HERMANN GÖRING

*The highlight of the Reichs Party Days.
As Chief of the Standarte ""Feldherrnhalle"", Hermann Göring himself marches his unit by the Supreme SA Führer, Adolf Hitler, on the occasion of the Reichs Party Days. Their excellent discipline is a sign of their attitude.*

are the loyal and brave trained. We have to get prepared. The Inter-Allied Control Commission can go to the devil.

Day and night the Hauptmann is busy. The right man is in the right place, the first SA Führer is on duty. In early 1923 the major workload is fulfilled. On January 28th Hermann Göring presents to the Führer the lined up Sturmabteilung. They are a tough troop, standing in rows and ranks, completely the Führer's.

Times become more and more severe. Germany's political conscientiousness is growing day by day. In March, 1923 the French crossed the Rhine River, well-armed and in endless columns.

Nothing happened in Berlin. The center of the national resistance is Münich. The men of the SA, the War Flag of the Reich, the Freikorps Oberland, the volunteers who still incorporate the national will, and all the others are closer and closer to Adolf Hitler. At this time new conflicts are threatening the Reich. In Thuringen and Sachsen there is the red revolution; in Bavaria the Truppen of the Bavarian Army are sworn in by General von Lossow. Between North and South there is a new gap. On October 26th the Bavarian State Minister, von Kahr, rids himself of the German government.

Now it is time. November 9, 1918 will

always be the blackest day in German history. For this reason, five years later the Führer chose this day to eliminate the German dishonor and disgrace. However, the Lord wanted it a different way. Still there is no victory to see for the National Socialist storm banner. The German Nation is still not mature enough. Not only the enemy from the left is against the Movement, but also the people's reaction opposes the young independent Movement. Under the bullets of the reaction, the march to independence breaks and the first National Socialist revolt at the "Feldherrnhalle" breaks as well. Next to Adolf Hitler, Hermann Göring goes down, hit by a machine gun bullet. Loyal friends brought him to safety.

We know how Hermann Göring, after the re-foundation of the Party, immediately offered himself to the Führer again. How he personally participated in the struggle for power and therefore formed the basis to build a new Reich. His spirit is the old immortal SA spirit. The same attitude linked him to the union of the fighters in brown shirts. In the last few years when he received tasks of more importance and responsibility from the Führer, he never found a more loyal and unselfish helper for the ideological propaganda to reach the goals of the four-year plan of the SA. They will never forget their first leader and he will never forget them.

*The SA Führer in Schliersee.
On September 30, 1923 a memorial for fallen Upper Schlesien men who were members of the union "Oberland" was held at the Upper Bavarian place of Schliersee. Hermann Göring also participated in this memorial as Führer of the SA.*

*U*nder the symbol of the sacrificial rune, which is for us National Socialists the incorporation of the highest willingness to sacrifice, the SA has formed a Trupp which is destined to symbolize the political soldiery of our time in the purest form, the Standarte "Feldherrnhalle". Already the fact that the Supreme SA Führer, Adolf Hitler, appointed his proven comrade, Obergruppenführer Herman Göring, as their chief, shows the mission of the Standarte today and tomorrow. As the central Trupp of the SA it is supposed to be an example in serving and obeying.

By this it is understandable that rules which the young team has to follow as they give their lives to the Standarte are very strict. Here only the best and healthiest of their race are chosen. Every year young men from all professions and levels join the central team. Of course, any differences concerning their origin or possessions are unknown. Here only the man is valuable, his efficiency and the obligation to be always ready and to obey his Führer.

All possibilities are open to those who prove well in the Standarte. After doing his one-year service he can make a decision to stay or go back to his profession. Also he has the possibility to get promoted to be a full-time SA Führer or join the administration services, of course depending on the applicant's capabilities and skills and the possibilities to use them in the political life of the Nation.

In six big camps all over the Reich hundreds of useable, efficient men are being valuably trained, whose political value cannot be shown by numbers or statistics. However, this is not what is most important. A lot more important for the justification of forming a political soldiery seems to be that from the school of the Standarte "Feldherrnhalle", National Socialists go out who are supposed to help

The first SA Führer - Chief of the Standarte
On his 44th birthday, Hermann Göring, Minister President and SA Obergruppenführer, was appointed Chief of the Standarte "Feldherrnhalle"; Stabschef Lutze himself brought him the appointment document as a birthday present. After a speech in which Obergruppenführer Göring expressed how much he was pleased to lead this central troop of the SA, he accepted the march past in front of the House of Flyers. Behind him is the Stabschef.

secure the creation which Adolf Hitler had started. That is why at the Standarte "Feldherrnhalle" the terms

Sentry duty is approved work
To be on sentry duty for two hours has always been the "most unpopular" duty. However, this sentry duty receives raised importance in the S t a n d a r t e "Feldherrnhalle", so they are not relieved any earlier from honor–duty or sentry–duty, although they stand still and must hold the look straight ahead. Whoever has done this for an hour knows what he has done. On the other hand, the sentry with a gun can walk around freely, and he will also be relieved after two hours.

An excellent parade march: good individual training.
Many concerns have been expressed about the parade march, actually exercise march, as precious training time which could be used on other issues. The men of the Standarte "Feldherrnhalle", who here are marching by their Supreme Führer at Nuremberg, are known to do the best parade marches in Germany, a sign of most diligent individual training and work where in a row only the whole is effective, and never the individual.

STANDARTE "FELDHERRNHALLE"

"Open the eyes – finger straight – pull the trigger!"
As central troop of the SA, naturally the Standarte "Feldherrnhalle" puts specific emphasis on shooting. That means to pull the trigger calmly, without closing
the eyes, and to hold the finger straight again. The SA gives excellently trained men to the armed forces.

Field service and training.
A major portion of the training is dedicated to field training. Every old soldier knows the so-called "crawling" which, especially in cold and muddy weather,
is no pleasure. Crawling means moving forward like a seal only by the help of the elbows, toes and knees, which are being moved sideways underneath the body
so that the man in the field is a no wider target than the width of his body.

"Question distance!"

In field service it is very important to get a good feel for distances. Also evaluation of the territory, language and sighting of the enemy. The territory always has to be evaluated properly, no matter whether attacking or defending, or already occupied by the enemy, or in case the enemy is firing. These are some among many truths. By intensive training the SA men learn how to act in the field and how to estimate distances, always by considering light and visibility, and also weather and terrain (for example mountains and coasts).

discipline, voluntary obedience, and soldier-like lifestyle are the first conditions in recruiting. Developed by the form of today's political life, copying the old, proven SA heroes, the Standarte "Feldherrnhalle" commits itself to the soldier-like way of life. It unites young men with a political consciousness who voluntarily want to live a life of hardship and soldier-like fitness.

Quick catastrophe service at all times.

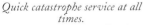

The volunteers of the Standarte "Feldherrnhalle" sacrifice many nights and spare time to do catastrophe service. Here a 100 meter long sugar factory close to Stuttgart burns. The photographer reported that the SA was still with the professional firefighters helping to extinguish the fire when he came back the next morning.

THE SA AT THE REICHS PARTY DAYS

A picture of monumental impression: Through the streets of Nuremberg marches the endless columns of the SA to the Adolf-Hitler-Platz.
Only a small number out of the SA participate in the Party Rally. Many see it as a unique event in their whole life for which they had saved money for weeks and weeks to be in Nuremberg at least once. "SA and Nuremberg" - this is a term that to this day ties the end to the fact that from the beginning the SA cleared the way to power for the Party.

Enviable perspective: From the best window spot in Nuremberg, these three girls watch the traditional marching of the SA.
Since the first Party Rally in Nuremberg, the SA marching in front of the Führer has been the highlight, and at the same time the end of these events, which shows the basic direction through the political fight, yesterday and today. From the beginning the SA put their revolutionary mark on the Party Rallies and showed to the world the picture of the fighting troops which were with the Führer in both good and bad days, ready to fight for a new future for the people.

One of many special SA trains arrives.
Often there are many hours of exhausting travel between departure and arrival at Nuremberg, and even then the exertions are not over with; on the contrary, now they just start when camp life begins at SA Camp Langwasser where the units are trained for the marches.

The history of the National Socialistic Movement is related to the development of its strongest structure. The fighting years proved impressively that the strongest arm of the Party, the SA, was able to complete the penetration of the National Socialistic idea into the people, as these troops have already become what the Party had to fight for for more than a decade, the political community of all Germans.

Better than each theory, the years behind the SA showed that only strict idealists make the contents of the training their confession of faith. Those who joined the SA lived a dangerous life. There was nothing to win and everything to lose. During the hardest years of German history there were days and stations where they could stop, which gave time to contemplate for a few hours. These days were the Party Days of the NSDAP. And they still exist as the holidays of a once laughed-at opposition which have become the highest holidays of the whole Nation.

Of course, much has changed since the first Party Day. From the outside the picture has become a hundred times bigger. More marching fields have become arenas of monumental size. The familiar impressions of the first Party Days still stick with the old ones, but we all feel that the sense of the big public holiday has remained the same. When the SA today and in the coming years marches in Nuremberg, when they annually renew their oath of faith to the Supreme SA Führer, they go back to work strengthened by new slogans, so this is more than an external thing. The SA, supported by their traditions, hardened during the fights with

Left: Order is mandatory!
During a break, the train station is being cleaned up. Orderliness and discipline are the first SA basics.

The Stabschef at Camp Langwasser.
Frequently and with pleasure the Stabschef stays at the SA camp during the Party Rally to spend a few hours of true and cordial camaraderie with his friends from all areas of the Reich.

The highlight of the Reichs Party Days is the roll call of the National Socialistic fighting units at the Luitpold Arena.
Annually more than 100,000 men of the SA, SS, NSKK and NSFK wait for an impressive rally, and in the presence of the Führer the virtue is sworn to the National Socialistic Party for victory though sacrifice and persecution. In this political demonstration Adolf Hitler speaks to his co-fighters and gives them trend-setting fighting slogans. Memorials for the dead during the roll call at the Luitpold Arena close the circle of the living with those who have fallen for the size and power of the new Reich.

artistic, significant educational tasks, demonstrated in Nuremberg for the old but always new mission of the National Socialistic ideas for which realization it once lined up.

That's why the columns of the SA belong to the Reichsparteitag, to its strong impressions, to its big and small pictures; that's why the SA and the Party Day have become one. When the columns of the SA annually march on the historic ground of Nuremberg they are aware of the fact that they are witnesses of a big time to a new future.

This handshake is a commitment!
In the presence of many thousands of political fighters, the Stabschef renews the SA's oath of faith to the Supreme SA Führer.

SA PUBS AND THEIR HISTORY

The "Wurzerhof" in Münich.
In Münich, the capital city of the Movement, the SA was christened. From there the incredible victory run of the brown Sturmabteilungen has its origin. At the "Wurzerhof" the old comrades from the time of struggle still meet today. The "Wurzerhof" is the oldest SA meeting place in Münich.

Here spoke Horst Wessel.
In Berlin where the political fight was extremely heavy, the pub owners who gave a place to the SA men and their Truppen (troops) had nothing to laugh about. As witness to this are bullet holes, smashed windows and the owner's pitiful financial situation. Some of the pub owners had to pay for their loyalty with their life, not to speak of their businesses being ruined. The specific target of the commune was the pub "Wiener Garten"; here spoke Horst Wessel. The interior clearly proves that the SA did not prefer luxury restaurants. Simple, clear, bright and friendly were the SA pubs.

Here Erich Sagasser was stabbed.
The SA pub "Erich Sagasser" on Havelberger Strasse in Berlin saw many bunches of flowers. The Sturm of Standarte 2 named it for him and quickly put up a few wreath decorations and his picture as a memorial to one of more than 40 SA martyrs who made way for the conquest of red Berlin. The night before Christmas Eve, Sagasser was stabbed here. It was a very sad Christmas celebration for his comrades.

Eberhard Maikowski.
When Hans Eberhard Maikowski led his men through Charlottenburg on the night of the takeover of power, Communistic motorcycle patrols had initiated a relay message service to the red highwaymen, who opened well-planned fire from the rear. At the beginning of this attack, the young activist fell, next to him Police Master Sergeant Zauritz. This happened close to his own pub.

The Mentor and Host of Haidhausen.
Among the innkeepers who, without considering the consequences, very early on became National Socialists, there also is Vater (Father) Semmelmann of Haidhausen in Münich, holder of the NSDAP Honor Badge. On December 6, 1925 the first Section meeting took place in his pub, and three times the Führer was there too.

A windy corner.
The SA pubs were ardently hated by the Marxists, as they represented a power and propaganda center. On this spot young Hermann Thielsch was shot on September 9, 1931.

Where the Führer spoke.
Today they are still sitting together, the men of the 10th Company of the SA Regiment, and speak of past days of fighting, sacrifice and victory, and into the future they lead the tradition as memory for the younger ones, whose example they were supposed to be.

"SA - Out"!

Very often a rock came through the window or a bullet splintered the wood on tables and the ceiling, by those who had opposing political thoughts; however, in reality, they were criminals from the underworld who through windows and doors were attacking while the SA men were peacefully meeting with their comrades, or were bent over their propaganda work, or were working on projects for the legal conquering of red strongholds. Then usually you heard a loud whistle and someone yelling "SA - out"! Some were fatally injured during these incidents or took a bullet in front of the pub. Some are still suffering from these injuries today.

THE DEVELOPMENT OF THE UNIFORM

1922

1923

1921

FLECHTNER

1923

When the Führer started to fight the criminals in Germany, he created a small Trupp which was supposed to secure for the young Movement those possibilities of public activities which were required by the propagandists and speakers in order to successfully perform their tasks. Soldiers who had returned from the horrors of war, students, handymen and workers surrounded Adolf Hitler in small numbers, in order to start the almost hopeless work. Initially the Führer called them Organizers, but after the first decisive battle in München, he proudly called them the Sturmabteilung.

Since then the SA man has put his stamp on the political fight in Germany. The very few individual fighters increased to hundreds of thousands, and became the army of the political soldiery of the National Socialistic Movement. The

form of their service, their responsibilities and their tasks have changed. The spirit remains the same.

The SA man wears his brown shirt, convinced that the new political idealization also creates the appropriate external forms and symbols. It is no coincidence that the first SA men were still wearing the old war uniforms. National Socialism received its creative forces with the help of the war faithful. That's why the gray uniform was the SA man's comrade for a little while, until the major tasks created the need for new uniforms. The brown shirt with the armband and the storm cap generally made its own way. Old, certainly preferred clothes had to give way to new requirements.

Similar is the development of our badges and flags. The first Sturmfahnen (storm flags), which had already begun to be destroyed, represented to the fighters in brown shirts the banner of the new idea. Gradually the opponents became accustomed to our accomplishments as matters of fact and to take us seriously. And this was important. The SA, as the strongest arm of the Movement, had made itself a political presence and the opponent could count on that.

Little changed concerning uniforms and badges after taking over power. The best tradition of the Party is still incorporated into the traditional uniforms of the time of struggle. New men joined the old fighters. Their symbols are stamped on our time. The political uniform of the SA dominates the picture of political life.

Are we mourning concerning old things like old spinsters about their missed opportunities? No way! The clothes and symbols have changed a little. Loyalty to the old flag and old uniform have remained the same. Whoever swears loyalty to them, takes it to the grave.

The fight for the new Reich, need, and hardship put a stamp on the face of the political soldier.
The "Standartes" of the SA, which were consecrated by the Führer himself, are symbols of struggle, but also of victory. Many carry the names of murdered SA men and the carriers also include the oldest and most efficient fighters in brown shirts.

In the political fights, the marches, rallies and deployments, the SA consciously shapes a new type of German man, the political soldier, who educates the people by his excellent attitude and involvement in accordance with the National Socialistic ideology. To be an SA Mann is not a profession, but a vocation, which does not bring him any advantages, but double and quadruple tasks. From all levels of the Nation come the men who are marching side by side, wearing the same brown outfit, and also internally equipped in their willingness to work. The spirit of the community and the service for the German Nation are the mottos under which they fight. This SA spirit always will be the same, as well as the big task which was given to the political soldiers by their Supreme Leader, the Führer Adolf Hitler. What changes is only the means and ways which will lead them to the goal, among which are both actions and public presentations, which is generally called service in the SA.

Only those who have experienced marching under the hot sun know how to appreciate a sip of fresh water. All participants appreciate the refreshments which members of the NS Frauenschaft and the BDM have ready for the teams who are competing carrying full packs.

The Supreme SA Leader, Adolf Hitler, surrounded by his SA comrades.
To each SA man the greatest experience is those hours he can spend with the Führer. The eyes of the men express their loyalty and perfect belief in his ideas while he talks to his comrades and gets familiar with their worries and needs.

TYPICAL CAMARADERIE PHOTOGRAPHS OF THE SA

Waiting for a turn to shave and comb.
These are two band members who the cameraman caught at their morning toiletté in the tent camp. Even though they don't have a big mirror on the wall, the most important thing is that the hair is in order.

Getting bread, this is the full-pack march that is gladly practiced.
Marching and field service make you hungry, but the emptiest stomachs will be filled again, and it even seems to be good. The men have big smiles on their faces in expectation of upcoming pleasures.

"If one of us is tired, the other will watch over him."
During the day they did their work standing behind a plow, or vise, or bent over the books, and at night they started traveling to Nuremberg. No wonder that two of them fell asleep while the third one was on guard.

"Soldiers will always be soldiers."
Every time, when men of one unit are together, you will hear the old and new fighting songs of the soldiers, no matter if they are marching through the streets of towns and villages, or are among their comrades. All through the SA songs is an appeal which wakes up the mellow ones and rallies the spirit of the political soldier.

TYPICAL CAMARADERIE PHOTOGRAPHS OF THE SA

A fresh drink served by gentle hands is twice as good.

After the SA had broken the terror of the subhuman in the streets of the German Reich and you heard their marching and songs all over the freed cities and towns, the grateful Nation joyfully welcomed them everywhere. The pressure which had been on the people for fourteen years, the worry for the future, and the uncertainty was taken off them and they knew who they had to thank in the first place. Under the impression of the System Era the enthusiasm was the greatest shortly after the taking over of power, an enthusiasm which showed itself in many ways.

While others were doing pleasurable things on Sundays, the SA marched and conquered Germany for the Führer.
At that time, in the year of fighting for power in the Nation, each propaganda march of the SA not only meant to do a tiresome service from voluntarily assumed responsibility and internal persuasions, but at the same time a constant threat for the men who, unarmed and carrying only their National Socialistic ideology, prepared the way for a new Germany, both in the country and in the cities. Some who in the morning were joyfully marching with their comrades did not come back, and others by evening were lying in hospitals, severely injured. However, their determination remained the same and for each dead fighter a thousand others jumped in, until victory.

EQUESTRIAN SA

In Germany nowadays the equestrian sports are no longer done by just a few professionals, but now, as has been the case for centuries, by all of those who are committed to horses and riding by enthusiasm and passion. We have the SA to thank, who made equestrian sports a means of physical training for the people.

None other than the Supreme SA Führer himself created the basis for this by issuing his decree of March 17, 1936 concerning the setting up of the National Socialistic Rider Korps. This served to bring the SA Equestrian and German youth old enough and capable of serving, above all people to the equestrian sports. This decree soon created the organizational conditions for the fact that the SA nowadays can give thousands of young trained riders to the riding and driving Trupp sections of our armed forces every year. The Führer's decree says: "All 18 to 20 year olds, as well as younger and older ones who are eligible for riding and driving training prior to the service, and want to get their riding certificate in order to serve in a riding or driving Trupp, have to join the NSRK." Further, it says: "The NSRK is formed of Equestrian SA, which includes approximately 80% of the German riders."

The Equestrian SA riders have to know this also.

A real rider has to know a lot more than riding itself. Whoever wants to become a real Equestrian SA has to learn at the same time how to take care of the horse in all respects, feeding, maintaining, brushing, grooming, bridling and saddling. The National Socialistic Equestrian Korps not only teaches how to ride and drive, but also trains the young rider in all things which have to do with true riding. Only then is the riding and handling of the horses really fun, when he himself is capable of doing everything which an experienced rider has to do.

Year by year the Equestrian SA competes in the most difficult German riding and jumping tournaments.

Courage, persistence, patience and tenacity - whoever does not have these virtues will not get far in the Cavalry. In the SA no so-called "Sunday" or "gentlemen" riders are being trained. The SA man in the saddle is a fighter; riding and jumping are not just a hobby to him. Equestrian sports are tough military sports. This picture proves it. It shows Sturmführer Herbert Frick of the SA High Command on the occasion of the German jumping derby in Klein-Flottbek, who only lost in the final round.

That was well done!

In the pentathlon for SA Führers, jumping became a duty. This means practicing and practicing again until the jump over the obstacle really is perfect. Whoever knows how to do it may rightfully say then that he is firm "in all saddles".

The organization of the NSRK is headed by the Reichsinspekteur for Riding and Driving, Obergruppenführer Litzmann, who directly reports to the Stabschef of the SA. At the same time he heads the newly created Main Office for Riding and Driving Education in the SA High Command. This way a very close relationship between those organizations has been created and in it is the fruitful cooperation between the SA Cavalry and the NSRK. In each SA Gruppe the position of a Gruppe Riding Führer who reports to the Reichsinspekteur has been created, and he is responsible for education and organization. Nowadays the SA Cavalry has 101 Equestrian Standartes, and their schools now train young Germans every year and enable them to join any Trupp they want.

By creating the Riding Certificate, the NSRK has found a method to maintain and advance riding abilities. Only those who meet all requirements and pass the riding exam receive the Riding Certificate. The Riding Certificate is also a method of selection and advancement of the really talented.

The NSRK is still young, but two years of serious work appear justified. Their successes prove the rightness of the way. Our SA riders are present in all tournaments today. They have advanced to be in the top class of the best German riders and by this have honored the SA. It is understood, of course, that the proud beginnings of our young SA Cavalry is the motivation for new struggles and victories, whose best and deepest sense lies in the fact that they all want to be an example and model to those who are devoted to riding by passion, enthusiasm and dedication.

Not for Sunday riders!
It takes courage to cross a river by horse. Whatever the SA rider learns during his training in the SA, he won't have to learn again when he is in the armed forces. Crossing rivers is frequently practiced during military maneuvers.

With man, horse and boat across Müeggelsee. (Müeggel Lake)
On the occasion of an exercise at Müeggelsee, the Berlin Equestrian SA, along with SA Engineers, show how a fully occupied boat can be moved by using the power of swimming horses. This picture shows in a pleasant way the possibility of useful cooperation of the specials units, in this case Equestrian and Engineer.

The German Equestrian Führer Badge.
On February 24th the Führer presented this badge, which is given for exceptional decisions and performance.

The Honor Badge for Merit in the NS Rider Korps.
The Führer presented this badge to deserving supporters of the NSRK work.

Setting sails on the jib boom.
It is not easy to set sails on the wildly jumping jib boom when the sea is heavy. This boom, on which the sails are being set, is frequently under water during storms. It is held to the bottom by the water stay and the lower chain, to the top by the four sails. It's sails make the big sailing ship faster and more aerodynamic. Of course, each man in the Naval SA knows the rigging and knows how to handle the ship.

Among the many uniforms you see on the streets, you relatively rarely see the man wearing the navy blue hat and coat, the Naval SA man. The men of the coastal areas who are seamen, fishermen, etc., mainly serve in the Naval SA so they can have something to do with water in their daily tasks. Nevertheless, Naval SA Standartes are not only on the sea but also inland,

for example, in Dresden. There are no big ships, but for theoretical training, frequently a so-called "landsailer" is sufficient, a ship which was reproduced as before with masts, shrouds, superstructures, etc.

It is clear that the service of the Naval SA has a completely different appearance due to its goal. Put simply, it is preparation and advancement for

the Navy. Signal duty (flagging, radio, Morse code, signaling), ship duty and seamanship (cutter pulling and sailing, navigating, astrology, etc.), skilled handling of a sailing ship, knots and splicing, and lifeguard duty are on the schedule, to mention only a few of the tasks. However, in the Sailing Standarte, whose men are scattered all over the world's oceans, is

Knots and splicing.
For each seaman it is of great importance to make a knot in a way that it can be quickly undone, even though he has to face each requirement. His life often depends on it. There is a weaver's stroke knot, stopper knot, stern knot, post knot, half knots, round knots, tuck splinters, carpenter's knots, etc. Mostly it is the voluntary watch that are learning how to make "knots and splices" while the ship is being navigated.

"Haul in the sails"
When riding with the wind the sails can be hauled in the best when the sails are "killing" according to the technical term. That means mostly when the ship is changing the stay sail, when it is turning. In a storm it is pretty dangerous; some can tell you stories about how their cheeks were slapped by heavy sails and the main sail was popping like a machine gun. Here the only remedy is packing quickly. Whatever the seaman packs like this, he doesn't let go.

"Saved!"
Frequently enough the Naval SA have risked their lives in order to save people from emergency situations. Here a man was saved by using a port buoy with which the threatened man was pulled from the wreck to the shore.

Only for people not afraid of heights.
The work of the men in the masts, sometimes up to 40 meters above deck, is a brilliant training, a courage test, an exercise for self confidence and facing dangers. In an icy snow storm, in rain and cold, it is no easy thing to bring in the very heavy sails with cold and frozen fingers. Many have gone overboard and disappeared in the sea. This is the fate of a seaman!

in the first place the ideological involvement of the men on board, which also shows abroad on the occasion of celebrations, marchings, etc. The Naval SA gives excellent pre-trained material to the German commerce and Kriegsmarine.

The Signal flag.
Training in the Naval SA, which mostly consists of active, weather-hardened seamen, also includes the signal service: Signaling, radio, Morse code, flag hoisting. In case of enemies approaching, at first they use signal flags even when radio and the morse code branch would seem to be called for. This man is just giving the letter "S" ("Sophie").

"And now the last 200 meters!"
The so-called "Cutter race", the rowing competition, requires long training of the team. In all German navigation the greatest value is ship duty, as it is the best conditioning to quickly and safely rescue the passengers in case of a sea emergency. The Naval SA especially likes this branch of navigation. On the occasion of the annual races, the men show how strong, young and supple their bodies are. (In the background: the Aviso "Grille" of the Kriegsmarine.)

THE SPECIAL UNITS OF THE SA

In the shortest time the Engineer SA secures river crossings and other obstacles.
The most important help equipment for passing wide, deep and quiet waterways are ferries and rafts. Logs are being laid over some pontoons and boats, then they are mounted and covered by boards. Quickly and safely the men are working, and soon the first part of the unit can be transported. Whatever they learn and practice during their daily duties will find its fulfillment on the occasion of catastrophe involvements, where SA Engineers give valuable help.

As the small combat patrol of the National Socialistic idea became an organization in whose hands the Führer laid the total physical and ideological education of our Nation, in the same mass was also growing the scope of the brown army of Adolf Hitler, which required the special training of units who were capable of prompt action and top results in their special fields. The Engineer Sturmes were developed. Communication Sturmes were set up. Since their creation, both units have proven again and again that the men with the "Pi" and the "Na" written on the badges of their uniform are to be found where the German people need their help. When a storm is agitating the waves of the sea and masses of water are threatening the coasts of the Reich, when rain floods and snow melting make mountain rivers swell up and fields and properties are threatened, when fire is about to destroy German possessions, or when natural catastrophes are spotted in all areas of the Reich, at these times you will find the Engineers and Communication engineers among the first helpers, pleasant and willing to sacrifice. However, SA duty is nothing for them other than duty for the people. The next morning you will find a brief report in the daily news and those who read this report while having a cup of morning coffee, are interested to learn that the SA helped again; however, only very few know what exactly happened during those hours of extreme struggle with the natural forces. Also they may not know that the same men who maybe spent the whole night giving their best are at their workplaces very few hours later, and very, very few really know what a thorough and proper education, what hard practice was necessary in order to be successful in the case of a catastrophe. And during these exercises we see bridges being quickly built, we see how blasting is performed and, in addition to the Engineer's services, we are amazed by the Signals units who are working hand in hand with them and who are laying field wires, mounting telegraphs, and linking speaking devices, passing messages on to others by bicycle riders, messengers or messenger pigeons, and making and securing connection briefly between the front and the staff, and on whose shoulders is a lot of responsibility in emergency cases. The educational status of the men of

The bridge is ready, the Sturm marches.
Beaten by the most simple technical means, the bridge does not only have to carry the men but also carriages and vehicles, in order to meet all requirements in emergency cases. Careful and constant training enables the SA Engineers to accomplish the highest achievements.

"Short-long-short" the device is blinking and passes the message on across long distances.
The involvement of the messengers, the men who are comprised in the Signals units of the SA, is of major importance for passing on commands and news. In the end of their training is the acquirement of the communications certificate, whose holders are preferred by the corresponding groups of the armed forces.

the Signals Sturme is subject to constant control by the Communications Certificate. This Certificate certifies that its holder can prove a considerable educational status. For three years in a row he has to pass subsequent exams until it is in the possession of the signalman.

This is what a field-ready telephone switchboard looks like.
The SA Signals man is not only supposed to be familiar with the radio, signal flagging and heliograph, but he must also be capable of setting up telephone lines quickly and under the most difficult conditions and to complete complicated connections. On the occasion of major SA performances, the men of the Signals staff show to the audience what they can do in case of emergencies.

THE SPECIAL UNITS OF THE SA

This way in these technical units of the SA a skilled team is developed whose abilities and knowledge are of extraordinary value in the service to defend the country. On one hand the young SA man who joins the Army from his organization already has a lot of basic training which makes his training easier in a technical way and speeds it up. On the other hand, those soldiers who have already served, who return from the field gray uniforms to the brown shirts of the SA, receive their educational status by constant physical and intellectual exercises. They pass their knowledge on to their comrades and therefore contribute to the increase of military power and thinking of the German Nation. However, nothing would be more wrong than to conclude from this fact that the SA is "playing soldier", because the SA and armed forces are and will remain two completely different supporters of the new State. Solely their final goal is the same, to serve the Nation and the State, and in reaching this goal, the soldier of the Army will find his closest ally in the political soldier.

Soon he will be on his way.
In addition to the modern technical assistance methods, today also the dog as loyal, four-legged friend of man, plays an important role concerning passing on messages. The messenger dogs of the SA Signals Service often do not belong to the men themselves, but are provided by their owners. Nevertheless, they show excellent training, which the public can witness for themselves on the occasion of the Reichs tournaments of the SA in Berlin.

Also in snow and fog, man and dog do their duty.
On the occasion of the SA ski meets of individual SA Gruppen, communications competitions took place. The goal was to set up multiple telephone lines according to indicated destinations for others. Here the messenger dogs, as well as the search dogs, were able to help safely reach the goal in poor visibility.

An SA Medical Sturme is marching.
The SA Medical Sturmes, which report to the Chief of the Main Office For Health, SA Obergruppenführer Brauneck, are involved on the occasion of all important Party events in order to render first aid.

lectual weapons", where everyone who was wearing a brown shirt was game, chased by white trash and the creatures of the system. At that time the SA medical personnel were the first ones to render first aid to the wounded and beaten bodies of their comrades, and who, frequently risking their own lives, brought others to safety, who did whatever they could, and whose willingness to help was more than once in vain, when their abilities were no longer sufficient in order to keep people alive. In times of struggle, the SA appreciates these medical men a lot. And these simple men became doctors for the body and soul and were known for being reliable in each situation. Even today when safety and peace are re-established, the SA medical men have not become unnecessary. Service in the SA and their continued willingness to act bring a lot of physical dangers with them but by acting promptly many injuries can be eliminated or improved. For example, heat, frost, accidents and some illnesses. The medical men are always available. They have to go through utmost hardships however, and in the case of catastrophes there are not enough doctors. The lives of many people depend on skilled help and treatment on the spot. Then the SA medical men give their best and act promptly. Unmentioned and unknown, they do their duty as the spirt and tradition of the structure requires.

Accidents in SA service can never be completely avoided.
The multiple involvement of the SA on the occasion of brush fires, floods and other natural disasters, as also in military sports, always result in all kinds of injuries, which mostly are of a minor nature. However, they require immediate action. The SA Sanitätskorps, with its excellently trained men, always acts promptly.

Born out of the community spirit of the SA.
Health institutions in the individual units are very good throughout the whole Reich, even if a portable x-ray system is not always available, as the one in the SA home of the Berlin Standarte 2, which here is visited by the City President, SA Gruppenführer Dr. Lippert, together with State Senator Görlitzer and Standartenführer Kraus.

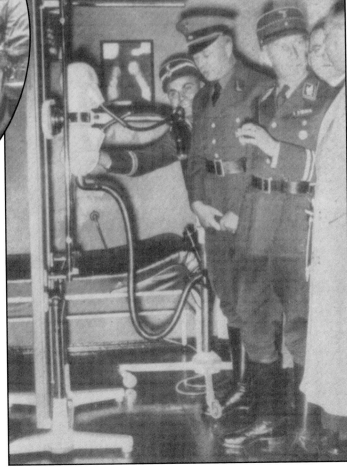

The SA medical men, our so-called Sani-Men, were there from the beginning when there were fights. Who would not recognize them, the men with the big bag and the Cross of Geneva on the white field. They were marching in each Sturme, yesterday and today. This was in those years where the red mob was waiting in the streets, where knives, pistols, brass knuckles, and rubber truncheons of the Marxists criminals were "intel-

When the Führer announced the re-establishment of general military duty, the SA thanked him by action. This action was one more proof of the sacrificing spirit of this Trupp. The present of the SA to their Supreme Führer, which was presented by the Stabschef on his 46th birthday, was a squadron of fighters. They had no more than ten days to make this idea, which was borne in the rows and spirit of the brown army, a reality. Within these ten days, however, the almost impossible was

In the spirit of the SA.
The Führer inspects the machines of the Horst Wessel Wing. Each of the airplanes carries the name of a murdered fighter out of the rows of the SA.

Their spirit has always been the proudest weapon of the political soldier and also this work.

The big moment has come.
The Führer is going to take command of the Horst Wessel Wing with the Stabschef, the Supreme Commander of the Luftwaffe, SA Obergruppenführer Hermann Göring, other high ranking officers of the Luftwaffe, and the Gruppenführers of the SA.

Right: The willingness became the action.
With his brief soldier-like speech, the Stabschef gives the Hunting Wing to the Führer as a miliary present of the SA on April 20, 1935, his 46th birthday. This is evidence of the military willingness and readiness of the leaders and men of the SA to sacrifice for the Führer.

made possible. Each of the men contributed, but this contribution was not a simple donation for most of them, it meant a sizeable sacrifice. This present of the SA not only served the military forces of the new Reich, is not only a symbol of love and loyalty to the Führer, but above all it is the fulfillment of a will, which we owe to the murdered comrades. And so each aircraft of the three squadrons of the Hunting-Wing "Horst Wessel" has an approximately plate-size symbol on its fuselage bearing the name of one of our comrades who

fell for the future of the Reich. A new bridge was built between soldiers of the Luftwaffe and the SA by this gift, even though both were already related by the same spirit and through the Supreme Commander of the Luftwaffe, Generaloberst Hermann Göring, who at the same time was the first leader of the SA and now is SA Obergruppenführer, Chief of the SA Standarte ""Feldherrnhalle"". The main seat of the squadron is the airbase at Dortmund-Brackel. The whole orderly flight base spreads high spirits and posi-

tiveness. The spirit of the Army of the new Reich speaks through it and its soldiers, based on the tradition of the field-gray Army, now fueled by the drive and force of the National Socialistic ideas. Neat, bright and roomy are the housing areas for the men and officers. A sports arena, as well as a nice outdoor swimming pool, make sure that the young men have everything they need for physical exercises. However, the SA will make sure that the flight recruits taken out of their ranks will be made capable of top results by military training.

THE RELIEF ORGANIZATION NORTHWEST BUILT THE WALLBERGSTRASSE

High above the Tegernsee (Tegern Lake), the SA comrades of the Relief Organization camps built one of the most beautiful mountain roads in Germany. Nature and technology are united in this work of proud and unselfish SA spirit. In six huge curves, the road, beginning at Oberach, climbs the northwest hillside of the Wallberg where the steepest increase of 13% passes a height difference of 750 meters. The five-meter wide road has been widened to ten meters in the curves. Passing steep canyons and high forests, the driver reaches a height which, until a few years ago, was reserved only to the mountain climber.

Left: Equipped only with minor technical means the SA comrades bring the road to the mountain.

Above: The result – the completed road is steeply winding up the Wallberg.

This highest mountain road in Germany was built by the SA for their Führer, and therefore for the German Nation, out of impeccable loyalty and readiness to act and stands as a memorial at the Wallbergstrasse in the area of the Tegernsee (Lake Tegern), close to the border between the Reich and Austria. One of the most beautiful mountain views in the Bavarian Alps was made accessible to through traffic by men who were members of the SA Gruppe "Hilfswerk Northwest" who executed and completed this immense project after two years of hard work. The difficulties seemed almost impossible when the order to start the work was given on September 1, 1935. A long existing former plan with high costs had always failed when attempted, but the SA comrades wanted to make it become a reality. They wanted? When the SA wants something they make the idea become a reality. That is what happened here, too. You should not forget that only extremely simple means were provided and therefore almost all technical equipment which was usually provided for the execution of such a work had to be replaced by manpower in this case.

Through tough, hard work the road was built meter by meter, and climbed higher and higher up the 1,722 meter high mountain until the Wallberg house was reached, which is 1,500 meters above sea level. Proudly the men can look at their result and with them the whole SA, whose spirit here made come true an unforgettable site and memorial. However, the 750 comrades who worked here for two full years as laborers and engineers, technicians and masons, architects and Party leaders, who by this project created in each respect an eight kilometer long mountain road, returned to their daily duties after completion of their work, unknown soldiers of work, unknown SA men.

Mountain men at work.
Here they are working at Curve Number 4, one of many beautiful curves and passages through the marvelous area of Tegernsee (Tegern Lake).

Above: Stabschef Lutze on the occasion of one of his tours of the construction work in the summer of 1937.

Right: On steep rock walls the men drove the rock drill into the hard stone in order to bore the holes for the explosives.

THE REICHSFÜHRER SCHOOL

Books – weapons of the political fight.
A library containing many thousands of books where in first place are political and histor-ical books which serve the ideological education. Of course, the literature of the Movement has a special place here.

the Reichsführer School of the SA in Münich, which was created by the Führer in 1931. Many thousands of SA Führers were instruct-ed and trained here who then went to their units at the front of the present political fight, provided with knowledge and ideological information, in order to pass their experiences and newly won impressions on to those who have to keep them. The work of the Reichsführer School of today is focused on bringing the synthesis of body, spirit and soul closer to the ideal. All technical means are used. In nine-month training courses the SA Führer recruits are introduced to all fields of political life. However, this is not happening in accordance with past school methods, which merely made the quantity of the teaching material the sole content of their

They don't make it easy for an SA Führer recruit.
At a Reichsführer school the young leader recruits receive the finishing touches in all educational branches of the SA service. The SA Führer needs to be able to first do himself what he demands from the SA man. The task he just received doesn't seem to be too easy. The comrade's face shows it.

Those who want to lead have to have learned to obey. The SA - the Stosstrupp (combat patrol) of the German Revolution - has made these findings the basis of their political actions in the years of the political fight. During the bloody hall fights in the big cities and the propagandistic attacks on the political fortresses of our opponents, the leader's principle had to prove itself. At the time that the SA had its breakthrough they wanted their leaders to be examples of how they had learned to obey as required by the National Socialistic program.

The time after the struggle for power advanced these findings. The new possibilities resulting after 1933 where systematically used according to proven examples in order to build a leader korps within the SA which in all respects met the requirements which the Führer him-self considered to be the conditions for the eternal exis-tence of his Movement. Selection of leaders and educa-tion of the leaders per the plan - this was the new way which, after taking over the power, was in included in the circle of the political work of the Party.

An effective instrument for such leader training is

Imagine the enemy is on hill "A". You and your Sturme are in fortress "B". What would you do in order to....
When it comes to action tasks, the SA Führer has to be capable of acting quickly and cautiously. In emergency cases, as well as with facts, his decision has to be precise and clear. Here practical action tasks are explained using a big relief map. The instructor only interferes in the presentation in case of any mistakes. This is because the Führer recruit has to be trained to think all by himself.

This is healthy and makes you hungry.
The form of military sports of the SA has developed its own form. The task to physically train the whole Nation, which the Supreme SA Führer wanted the SA to do, not only requires theoretical knowledge of sports methods by the SA Führers, but also the practical execution of those exercises which the SA made the means of total physical training.

In the circle: Physical training at minus 8 degrees.
SA sports are not for the occasional sportsman! In the sports arena at the Reichsführer School at Grünwald, which is close to Münich, they practice military sports in all weather. When the Führer recruit returns to his formation many are amazed at what he learned at the Reichsführer School.

The Stabschef on the occasion of the final exams of the class.
Usually the Stabschef is present during the graduation of each class in order to fully convince himself of the performance status of the Führer recruits and to say goodbye to them with a motivational speech.

schools where apprentice instructors are trained. The Reichsführer School wants to motivate the young SA Führer to creative work, to train him to think, and to form him to become a political personality of moral strength. Body, spirit, soul - one is not possible without the other. Hard physical training, strict measures concerning health and racial evaluation, and permanent surveillance of the style of life are valuable, but also unavoidable methods of strict and tough work. The hardest requirements are for those who are competent to guide young people as full-time SA Führers one day.

The second task of the Reichsführer School is to prepare the two-week work seminars for older unit leaders, from the leaders of the Standarte to the staff officials every year around the time following the Reichs Party Days. In these work seminars political balance during the past year is evaluated. So the Reichsführer School plays an important part in the political educational work of the Party. Maybe the results of the new leader recruit education will be visible in the following decades; however, even today you can clearly see the goal. A person who is National Socialistically trained, his spirit and body strengthened, has moral character.

THE REICHS MEDICAL SCHOOL OF THE SA

In the auditorium of the Reichs Medical School of the SA the participants are watching and listening with great interest and eagerness to theoretical essays to learn practical performances.

Picture sketch of the Reichs Medical School of the SA in Tübingen am Neckar, which is under construction.

Effective May 1, 1937 the former medical school of the Gruppe Südwest was appointed as Reichs Medical School of the SA by the order of the Stabschef. The appointment of this school to Reichs Medical School was the beginning of a unitary institution directly reporting to the Chief of the Main Office For Health of the SA High Command. Thanks to the generous cooperation between the SA and the University of Tübingen, this institution, under its director, Medical Standartenführer Holtgrave, became very important.

The development of this school shows the importance of the task which the Führer gave to the SA in addition to physical training and all related health questions. Good health care, corresponding to military willingness and thinking, cannot be performed by people who do not know anything about this idea, but only by comrades who are connected to the caretakers by shared experiences. This medical institution of the SA, in addition to its purely military medical tasks, is almost completely included in the service of health care and maintenance of the public and the military. The motto for the medical man is to fight for the renewal of the German human being. Technical knowledge and skills, in addition to action to maintain the people's health, make an SA medical man always ready. The SA-like education based on the virtues of the soldier, the SA-like training, and the extensive training in medical services and healthcare make the medical man going through the Reichs Medical School of the SA useful. To be a propagandist of healthcare and always ready to act.

To the strongest extent the Stabschef takes care of the Reichs Equestrian Führer School and the education of the rider recruits of the SA.
Heading a seminar, Stabschef Lutze (middle first row) participates in a riding excursion to the surroundings of the school at Berlin-Zehlendorf. To the left next to the Stabschef, is Obergruppenführer Litzmann, the Reichsinspekteur for Riding and Driving.

lead the training of the Standartes and Sturmes they are responsible for in accordance with mutual ideas. Those participants who, due to their leadership qualities, especially stand out to be riding and driving instructors, receive the so-called "German Equestrian Führer's Badge", presented by the Führer and Reichs Chancellor.

The Führer of the Reichs Equestrian School is SA Brigadeführer Lehmann who is assisted by excellent instructors, among them being Major Bürkner of the Cavalry Inspection, who heads the equestrian education. So with time the Reichs Equestrian Führer School creates the urgently required number of good instructors whose profession will serve the education of the Army.

The skills will decide.
An advanced seminar participant here shows an excellent jump in front of an audience.

Outside of Berlin, in Zehlendorf, close to the manors of people at historical Königsweg, there are the neat and practical buildings of the Reichs Equestrian School. In four-week courses here the Standarten and Sturmführers of the NSRK are gathered to receive necessary guidelines in order to

A picture of orderliness and discipline.
SA riders, participating from all Gruppen, are waiting for the Stabschef. The equipment of the school and its furnishings are excellent.

THE SA RETRAINING CAMPS

The practical training work at the retraining camps has begun.
These two men may have been in the crowd of the so-called unskilled workers which nobody knew what to do with, and who in the best years of their youth received neither employment nor a professional opportunity.

The economical morale of the democracy in 1918 left behind approximately seven million unemployed in the National Socialistic Nation. The sins of the system from 1918 through 1933 can be seen today in the feasible light of fully skilled special workers who meet the requirements of an industry in full operation.

A useful method to train the necessary number of specialized workers in increasing volume has been created by the SA at two lake camps. Camp Lockstedt of the Gruppe Nordmark and Retraining Camp Falkenstein of the Gruppe Sachsen have been busily working for a few years with diligence and dedication to this task. Already year by year thousands of skilled special workers are

The "new ones" are coming! Men, who in the best years the economical system of the Weimar Republic put on the street and excluded from the production process, are being retrained at Retraining Camp Falkenstein of the SA Gruppe Sachsen. All those who are eager and able can be trained to become a qualified skilled worker in two years and have the best job opportunities today.

transferred to industry to fill the gaps, which have threatened our work life for three or four years.

The purpose of the SA retraining work in the two major retraining camps can be described in very few words. The purpose is to give additional workers to the German economy. Germany may not have any more unskilled workers in the future. This is the goal ahead of us, and the SA, by using its methods and possibilities, has started to realize this goal.

Since the summer of 1935, so-called unskilled workers are being retrained in both camps thoroughly and diligently to become qualified and special

First is the "Great Theory".....then the practice.

In the two major retraining camps, Lockstedt and Falkenstein, slow and thorough work is being done, either according to theoretical or practical methods. According to modern requirements, formerly unskilled workers receive a training which enables them to be fully employed in professions which we have a practical lack of today. Nobody is too old. On the contrary, at the new job some will be young again.

This is fun: The most modern machines are available.

Thoroughness is law No. 1 at the SA retraining camps and only the most modern machinery is good enough to train these special workers. The beginning is always hard but this young man sees a task in front of him and his life makes sense again, and the German economy is waiting to receive this thoroughly trained recruit. This SA comrade will always remember his training at Camp Lockstedt.

Sports as activity to make up for hard labor.

Of course, SA service is never neglected at the training camps. Specific attention is paid to the men being physically fit, as this is essential for them to be able to endure hard professional exertion. Tenacity and fitness exercises to train the body are on the daily agenda of the camps.

In concentrated detail work the unskilled learn, in approximately two years, what it takes an apprentice three or four years to learn.
The practical work usually starts at the vise and for many it is work they are not used to. Anyway, many have not done work like this in several years. Carefully and thoroughly they are being retrained. Each detail is being explained and then practiced until they are familiar with everything. When these men apply their special skills on the job, they can cope with each particular task.

workers, which happens in cooperation with the Reichs Institute For Unemployment Benefits, the industry which supports them in a grateful way, and the SA High Command. The training and retraining work has been performed in accordance with the standards of the German Committee for Technical Schooling. Above all there are machinists, metal workers, precision mechanics, auto mechanics and electronic welders who have to be trained.

The training period is two years. Then the "apprentices" receive the journeyman certificate which enables them to be employed at an appropriate industrial factory. This certificate equals the ordinary apprenticeship certificate.

In addition, they receive ideological education and physical education in accordance with the approved methods of the SA Sports.

Today we cannot see how valuable this education is at both camps. Only in the future will we realize that the SA has done well to act in this decisive hour where they had to act quickly and thoroughly.

From "unskilled" to skilled worker is a long way.
Everything that has to do with retraining is available at the camps, from tools to special machinery, from optical instruments to metal forge, where you can hear from early in the morning until late at night the hammer blows of new work and a new future. However, above all is the comrade's willingness to make the sacrifices which made life livable again.

They experience Germany.
Explore Germany! The Adolf Hitler Free Resorts come true for many who have sacrificed their health while fighting for the Reich. Here we see visitors on holiday at old Dinkelsbühl.

A scream echoes through a city street filled by the dark of night. In the shadows of the lanterns disguised figures are disappearing. In a puddle of blood a man is in agony. Unconscious, blood all over him, he is lying in the pale twilight. Then a police siren can be heard through the night. An emergency vehicle receives the severely injured. The murderers are already in their hideout. The next day, the newspapers show an unimportant little article: "Last night an SA man was attacked and severely injured by unknown assailants."

This was five, six, eight and ten years ago. Like a bad dream this is all behind us now. Germany is a country of orderliness again. Eventually time will heal the wounds caused by the time of struggle. Much has been done already to get them out of the consciousness of those still

Long-awaited happiness: A vacation in the country.
Men, who for many years have sacrificed a lot and who forgot how to learn, find themselves again and also their happiness to be alive at the Hitler Free Resorts. Everywhere in the wide nation they relax, surrounded by comrades, who thank the old guard by giving needy comrades a free vacation.

suffering today. Law and order are the basis of the support system which takes the worry away from the old fighters.

Moreover, the whole Nation has an opportunity to show gratitude to the old guard of the Führer through the Adolf Hitler Free Resorts. For three years now this beneficial service sets about to make up for and do everything that needs to be done to heal the wounds of the time of struggle and to let the persons carrying the scars know that their sacrifices have not been in vain.

Vacation as an adventure.
Of course, vacationers are also made familiar with the characteristics of the landscape, cultural monuments, intellectual creativity and economical life.

The old fighters want neither benefits nor sentimental pity. They were fighting as their hearts told them to do for the Reich. Even today they don't expect any gratitude or pay. They

AT THE ADOLF HITLER FREE RESORTS

This is the way that we thank the old guards of Adolf Hitler that did the fighting for Germany.
In the last few years it has become a nice tradition that every year thousands of old deserving fighters receive a free vacation. The organization of the Hitler Free Resorts, which is sponsored by the NSV, within a short time has become an institution whose blessings we don't want to do without any more. Many thousands of comrades have found their joy of life and creativity through its existence. The scars of those who fought during the time of struggle start to heal, and the people from beyond the borders and with differences shake hands and become a nation.

did their service at the front of a new and nicer work, as in old times. Once a year, however, they think about how nice it would be if they could rest and relax, free from the worries of daily life and their job, far away from the ugly inconveniences of life. Many of the old fighters nowadays can travel and relax on their own. However, at least equally as many are dependent on the aid of others. Here the Adolf Hitler Free Resort Donation intervenes effectively. In cooperation with the SA units, it provides free vacations to their Organization in the Reichsleitung headed by the

One can feel at home here.
The German Nation knows what they owe to the old fighters. Friendly people and a nice home let them soon forget the past.

This resort is for the people's health. The SA resort Wyk on Föhr.
It is good to be here, we want to recover here. This house was given to the Führer by German officials, and Hitler gave it to his SA. From all areas of the Reich the vacationers come in order to regain energy for their daily work.

Light and air, sun and pleasure, which are free.
Gratefully this comrade, who here is cared for and protected by tender hands, will think back to the time which he spent surrounded by grateful comrades, far from his job and daily life and free from worries.

NSV in all areas of the Reich, and in the most beautiful areas in Germany, for old, deserving co-fighters of the Führer whose economical situation excludes a vacation at their own expense. For two to three weeks the vacationers live far from work and get to know a group of other people, get to know the German country, and maybe find the joy of life again.

The right to work includes the right of relaxation and vacation. Before, only the wealthier ones could travel. Nowadays, we have given the opportunity to relax to all working Germans. The free Hitler resorts make sure that above all, those who deserve it will get a vacation and rest. To whomever stood the test during the fight for Germany's independence, Germany is offered as their prize.

Those who favor the free Hitler resorts in order to eliminate existing injuries and deficiencies, indeed confess to practicing National Socialism. This, in addition, is to say that this organization represents an action of social self-help which is a non-profit organization, but fully supports those who have not speculated regarding results, profits or business, but who inserted itself in the hour of need to make Germany German again!

In the Bavarian Mountains.

The great educational sense of the Hitler Free Resorts is in the guarantee that it brings people closer to each other. The northerners come to the south and the people from the east visit the west. This way the whole Nation learns about itself again.

In the area of Baden.

The so-called "Hitler vacationers" are being concentrated in marching blocks made up of members of all structures of the Party.

"Hitler vacationers" are always cheerful. Far away is work and the dull daily routine. The marching blocks of the Hitler Free Resort in front of the Heidelberg Castle.

STURM "REICHSAUTOZUG DEUTSCHLAND" (REICHS AUTO CONVOY GERMANY)

The "Reichsautozug Deutschland" goes through Germany.
Provided with all technical means, the auto convoy "Germany" is available for all Party demonstrations. Also in the case of catastrophes and emergencies, the support convoy has been able to help efficiently.

Soon the command will be given.
Autos and teams are always ready to be utilized across the wide Reich. Be prepared is the motto for the crew.

Our Führer and Chancellor literally said on the occasion of the 10th anniversary of the first Party Rally in Coburg in October, 1935: "Without cars, without airplanes and without loudspeakers we never would have conquered Germany." We all know that the election results in Lippe in 1933 were decisive for the events which started to press upon each other from that moment on. A very important portion of the success is due to the loudspeakers. Former Sturmführer Schäfer of the Gruppe Niedersachsen had accumulated all available and attainable electric acoustical means on the occasion of this Party Rally in Lippe. He used to race from meeting to meeting to create great range for the voices of the prominent speakers of the Party. In appreciation of his efforts, former Sturmführer Schäfer was received by the Führer and made responsible for loudspeaker transmissions in the whole Reich. The Stabsleiter of the Propaganda Division of the Reich, Oberführer Fischer, tirelessly worked with Sturmführer Schäfer to speedily carry out the ideas. The SA may be appreciated for the major portion of the successes and services of the technical masterpiece, due not only to the creator and leader of the auto convoy, SA Brigadeführer Schäfer, but the whole team of the Sturm "Reichsautozug Deutschland".

The vow of loyalty.

Year by year the SA creates new leaders who, according to their abilities, are supposed to continue the old SA traditions and to fulfill their educational work in the German Nation. Educated by the newest methods, provided with a lot of knowledge, politically firm and hardened in character, the SA Führer Korps recruits start their work. Their mission is to be an example to the people; their obligation is to be loyal.

On top: Hermann Göring.

The highest SA Führer, Hermann Göring, who the Führer made responsible for big, important tasks, is still close to the SA today. As Chief of the Standarte ""Feldherrnhalle"", which incorporates political thinking and presentation of the SA at its best, Obergruppenführer Herman Göring represents the type of political fighter who gives his whole heart to our tasks and his whole life under the flag, which is the symbol of the new Reich. To be like him will always be the SA's highest rule and mission from the heart.

According to the Führer's will, the SA is eager, in addition to their political tasks, to bring their military spirit to the people, by attitude, being an example, and actions above and beyond. When they are successful, and I have no doubts, to maintain and strengthen the mental and physical military forces of the Nation, history will evaluate this second decisive victory as being higher than the first one.

Hermann Göring
Generalfeldmarschall

The work of the SA is to maintain the military National Socialistic spirit in their ranks, and most importantly to intensify the National Socialistic ideology in the nation. The Army wishes all the best for this work in the present and future.

Der Oberbefehlshaber des Heeres
von Brauchitsch
Generaloberst

Service in the Naval SA means considerable, versatile and valuable support for the Kriegsmarine. In addition to the ideological training and propagandistic effectiveness of the valid sea thoughts, its service is to maintain the military capability of the soldiers dismissed from the Kriegsmarine.

The names of the sailing training ships "Horst Wessel" and "Albert Leo Schlageter", both externally present the relationship between the Kriegsmarine and the SA. They will transfer the spirit of these volunteer fighters to the youth who are being trained to be men.

Der Oberbefehlshaber der Kriegsmarine
Raeder
Generaladmiral Dr. h.c.
(Honorary)

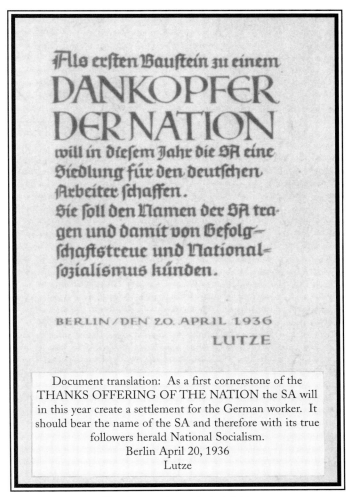

Als erften Baustein zu einem

DANKOPFER DER NATION

will in diesem Jahr die SA eine Siedlung für den deutschen Arbeiter schaffen.
Sie soll den Namen der SA tragen und damit von Gefolgschaftstreue und Nationalsozialismus künden.

BERLIN / DEN 20. APRIL 1936

LUTZE

Document translation: As a first cornerstone of the THANKS OFFERING OF THE NATION the SA will in this year create a settlement for the German worker. It should bear the name of the SA and therefore with its true followers herald National Socialism.
Berlin April 20, 1936
Lutze

A signature as gratitude and appreciation.
The Stabschef is the first to put his name on a petition for donations for the people in one of the Berlin-Zehlendorf Sturm pubs.

Year by year the results look better.
This is the second document for the practical gratitude of the Nation which donated 5.2 million in the first year and 8.6 million in the second year.

Everybody wants to give because the struggle was for them.
Those who contemplate this picture feel the fact again that the poorest sons of our Nation are also the most loyal ones. Here employees with rough work hands write their names on a contract. The letter of an SA man to the SA High Command was the cause for this collecting of money in the SA in 1935. The money was used for the Horst Wessel Wing as a birthday present for the Führer. The next year this appreciative action was extended to the whole Nation.

THE THANKS OFFERING OF THE NATION

The sign of old comradeship.
Our military comrades come in crowds to show their good relationship with Adolf Hitler's political soldiers. Some of them were wearing the brown shirts not too long ago. Brown and gray are one unit as military spirit results in military capability. The "Thanks Offering of the Nation" is not a collection from house to house; you have to go there yourself to sign.

direction you have to go to get to the sign-up place where a thick book of lists is waiting for your signature, then the famous action is on which Germany is right to consider a creation of the SA and which deserves the name "Thanks Offering of the Nation". The "Thanks Offering of the Nation" is one of the annual actions whose purposes are to train the SA Mann to be the best trained National Socialist, shoulder to shoulder with the whole Nation as part of this superlative creation of the Führer.

"Don't push – Everybody will have his turn."
In the Bolshevist Nation you had to line up in front of the food stores. In the new Germany you patiently wait until it is your turn to donate or sign for the "Thanks Offering of the Nation". The SA Gruppe Berlin-Brandenburg holds the record with 675,000 (1936) and 970,000 (1937) Reichsmark.

When heavy trucks which used to bring men to meetings as speakers, stage and house protection, are rolling through the streets of the cities and the rural areas, when huge banners are put up from house to house, advertising is being done, there are loudspeakers, crowds are shouting, music is playing the old songs, and when the big red arrows show the

This scoop of earth marks a new era.
An important day: Kitzingen, close to Würzburg, Feb. 28, 1937, the first cut with a spade for the second "Thanks Offering" area of the SA. In Dec., 1937 the first 96 houses were occupied in Germany. In the planning stages: 1,267. Under construction: 982 houses. The total is 2,345 houses on Dec. 31, 1937.

Front fighters and political soldiers.
Not only during the war they were doing their duties, they are still doing them and are proud to be
old, but always young, soldiers of the Führer. Their leisure time is still the smallest sacrifice in this service.

For some of them it is unfamiliar hard work – but who cares.
As soon as they put down their pens, tools or typewriters, they grab the spades to voluntarily create something for the Nation, as these SA men who make a sports arena out of a junkyard.

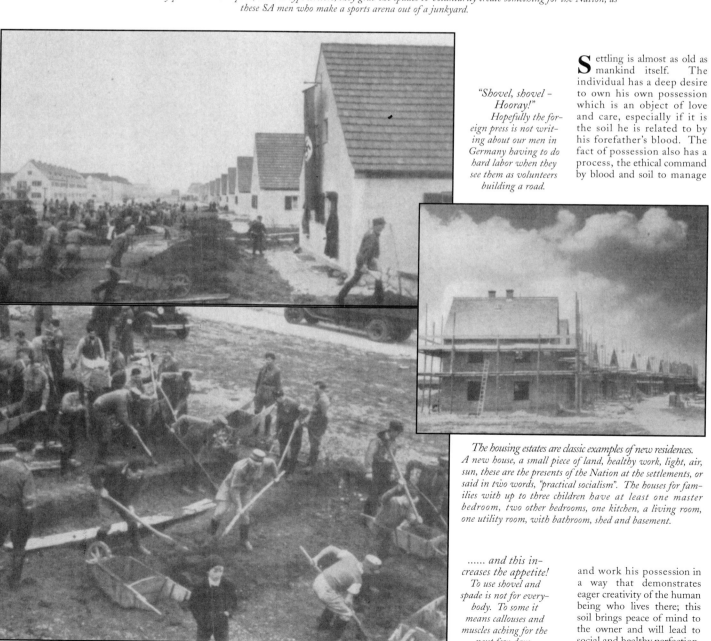

"Shovel, shovel – Hooray!"
Hopefully the foreign press is not writing about our men in Germany having to do hard labor when they see them as volunteers building a road.

Settling is almost as old as mankind itself. The individual has a deep desire to own his own possession which is an object of love and care, especially if it is the soil he is related to by his forefather's blood. The fact of possession also has a process, the ethical command by blood and soil to manage

The housing estates are classic examples of new residences. A new house, a small piece of land, healthy work, light, air, sun, these are the presents of the Nation at the settlements, or said in two words, "practical socialism". The houses for families with up to three children have at least one master bedroom, two other bedrooms, one kitchen, a living room, one utility room, with bathroom, shed and basement.

...... and this increases the appetite!
To use shovel and spade is not for everybody. To some it means calluses and muscles aching for the next few days.

and work his possession in a way that demonstrates eager creativity of the human being who lives there; this soil brings peace of mind to the owner and will lead to social and healthy perfection.

Caesar gave land to his old loyal legion soldiers as appreciation for their services. By doing so he also strengthened their loyalty, their health and social power, and at the same time in a military political way made a living wall on the borders of the empire. He literally built a wall of soldiers, who in times of emergency defended their plows using swords.

However, homesteading has a different meaning in a country where people are struggling daily with the region and the harvest god. Here you need a plan for homesteading in order to direct consumption and growth. The SA homesteading which has been made possible by the "Thanks Offering of the Nation" became a great social feat, as well as racial selection of the fighting manhood. Deserts have become productively cultivated soil, and out of this conquered land the new community of the coming nation is growing, whose fathers are active carriers of history for the Third Reich.

The miner at the Schlesischen mines and his many family members have received a gift from the comradeship of the great brown fighting community and by the willingness of the Nation to sacrifice, which thanks the Führer and his followers, a gift that put them in the position to see "light and sun, property and home" realized which had only been promised by the past system and which are the basics of National Socialistic politics.

It is a symbolic action when

Home, yard, garden – Everything is his!
The garden plots are 600 to 1000 square meters, according to the quality of the soil. Later on families with many children can build one to two additional rooms in the attic.

the whole German Nation builds a house for her loyal poor son and gives him land so that he has more from life. It is more than just a gesture when this Nation gives him a new home, a new roof, and a new Reich.

Those who have an interest in political actions and also in history will attentively follow the line of this new German homesteading plan by the SA, which will only show progress in the future. That is to say when the first hereditary carriers of the genes of this community will tend to take the reins of the horse out of the father's hand, tired by work and fight, and they harvest what their fathers have cultivated.

A homesteader's pride – The first harvest.
"See father, even though they are very young, in a few years from now we will have the first preserves!" Small domestic animals, garden tools, fruit trees, fruit shrubs and fertilizers are supplied free of charge to the settlement houses.

THE WAY OF ONE FIGHTER

More than two decades have passed since the day when our Nation was called to arms in order to defend the future of its children in the biggest of all wars. Twenty years! They do not include what world moving events, what misery they have led our Nation through; however, how wonderful the way of life has turned! The steel attacks of the battles have purified the front generation and those who got out of them uninjured have taken

Germany in their hands. The private first class of the war has advanced to the First Soldier and Worker of the Third Reich.

Nowadays we consider it almost incomprehensible good fortune that the people who had been at the front did not put their arms in their laps because they were tired and just let things go along, but they understood the signs of the times and again lined up to fight for the Reich under the flag of the political Movement.

The individual destiny of a soldier, an SA Führer, or a fighter in the line of fire of the political front of our days, is supposed to show us that victory was not without effort and struggle, and the station of a life full of struggles and sacrifices may be shown as a small sign of our appreciation to those who did their duty during the war, and then when they returned

Twenty years ago....
The camaraderie of the big war remained beyond death and fulfilled its meaning in the loyalty of those who were spared in the bloody fighting. Max Zankl created a memorial for three comrades who had fallen in the air war.

Drawing: Lazarus (according to a sketch by Max Zankl)

The assassination of Comrade Georg Hirschmann on May 26, 1927.
Max Zankl wrote: "On May 26, 1927, nine SA men were attacked by 30 to 40 Communists (later there were 400) on their way to a general roll call in the Humboldtstrasse in Münich. It resulted in a fight in which Georg Hirschmann was beaten and severely injured. He died in the hospital." These SA men were injured during the attack, however all, with the exception of Hirschmann, answered the roll call. The flag was spared from the attack of the Communists.

Memorial for the dead comrade.
In the summer of 1934, seven years after Georg Hirschmann's death, his comrades honored him by naming a former red sports pub in the Martinstrasse, "Georg Hirschmann Place"

At the West Front, 1917.
"...even if it was tough times, there was the certainty that next to me and behind me there were comrades strong enough to take the physical and mental pressure."

were again lined up in order to make Germany German again.

The München comrades know Party Comrade Max Zankl as one of the oldest SA Führers in Germany who conquered the red fortress of the Movement, Au-Giesing, with very few SA men.

Max Zankl went into the field as a reserve soldier at the end of 1914. On the western front he was a flight engineer, shaken by the changing decisions of the battles. The war came to an

The face of the German front-line soldier.
The film "Stosstrupp 1917" (Combat Patrol 1917) in which Max Zankl performed, showed this face, drawn by the dangers and steel thunderstorms of the war, to the whole world. It is the face of the front-line soldier who kept the world under control for four years and protected the home country.

end. Max Zankl returned to the betrayed home country. In the Rhineland he realized that the traitors had occupied the country. He refused to head his own team, a soldier's counsel. The homeland, the Bavarian area, sees him again. But even here the betrayal eliminated every order. The red revolutionists had their hands on it. However, there is one possibility - resistance. Civilian resistance is the only backbone at the time. Max Zankl is one of them. The assassination of Eisner is the signal that the hour of decision has come. In this way, a soldier is almost forced to join the first group of the German Worker's Party of Adolf Hitler. On February 22, 1922 he joins the Party. From this day on Max Zankl gave his life to the Movement. After the re-foundation of the Party in 1925, he received member number 129. With his joining of the 3rd "Hundredschaft" of the SA Regiment München, which later formed the 9th "Hundredschaft" headed by Hans Zöberlein, life became dangerous. The opponents were there trying to kill him, boycotting his business and his existence. On November 9, 1923 the betrayal at the

The political war has begun.
With terror and armed force, with murder and vicious nocturnal attacks, the enemy believed they would be able to stop the victory of our Movement. Hans Kiefer, an SA Man out of Trupp 9, headed by Max Zankl, was shot and severely injured by the Communists when going home.

THE WAY OF ONE FIGHTER

SA Men of Trupp 9 of the SA Münich, headed by Max Zankl, prior to the reorganization of the SA in the year 1926.
The year 1926 was of importance to the entire SA. The goal had been realized. Now the political army started to organize and to advance to the opponent's fortresses. In this picture we see a row of old co-fighters of the Führer: Hans Zöberlein; "Vater Jegg"; Party Comrade Köglmaier; the present State Secretary in the Bavarian State and Minister of Internal Affairs, Max Zankl. To the upper right in the first row: Georg Hirschmann.

"Feldherrnhalle" attempts to destroy the young believing Movement. They bring the Führer to the fortress. However, his followers wait outside until he returns.

He returns. The SA gets together again. Max Zankl takes over the direction of Trupp 9 of the Giesinger SA Au-Giesing - that is the red bastion of the community defending its position by all means! However, the SA makes its way, with Georg Hirschmann being the first victim. Max Zankl was severely injured many times. In these rough times the Führer himself takes care of him, takes care of everybody who is in need. His healing hand slowly heals the wounds.

So the year passed between the annoying political small war, between prohibition, terror, boycott and the manipulations of the system. But then the Day of Victory comes. Then the SA rearranges everything and blows the red crowd away. This is the most beautiful day in the life of these fighters for Germany.

With the old Sturmabteilung spirit in their hearts, they continue the new major work. Max Zankl goes back to his job

In the turn of life: An old fighter gets married and his friends wish him luck.
The terror of the opponents was broken, orderliness took the place of chaos and disorder. Now the old fighters were able to think about themselves again. Work was the new motto: working, believing and continuing the fight to complete the work.

again, which is the right step. The Führer calls his followers into responsible positions. Nowadays, Max Zankl, after having been an active SA Führer for fifteen years is Obersturmbannführer, in addition to District Master Craftsman, master of his profession, and Senator of the capital of the Movement. The Blood Order and the Golden Honor Badge of the Party are the exterior signs of his involvement for the Führer. Out in Neu-Harlaching in a housing area for old fighters, there is a modest house where Max Zankl found a home for himself and his family in his life full of fights and sacrifices.

However, no thought is given to relaxing. His life, in spite of everything, is before him. Life goes on, because now it has received a valuable meaning again.

So the Münich SA went to the Party Rally in Weimar in 1926.
"...when we got ready to go, we found out that we had no money. So our Party comrades from the local Gruppe Au-Giesing had to give their last pennies once again so we could be in Weimar."

In the family circle: work, work!
There was a time when we never had time. All of our concerns had
to do with the Movement. Nowadays we have even less time for our-
selves. We have a lot to catch up on as we missed a lot and none of us can
complain about having too little work.

There stays the old one.
Outside of the city, in the settlement of the old fighters in Neu-
Harlaching, Max Zankl has found a home and resting place in his work,
and experiences a rich and healthy life. There he continues to work, with
new goals.

The job demands its justice again.
Max Zankl is a sculptor of statues. Every free minute, every hour
he spends in his shop. From the experience of fighting for Germany he
gets the power for creative work.

IDEOLOGICAL INVOLVEMENT

For honor and freedom, for jobs and bread.
Almost daily the advertising pillars with their posters for election rallies and announcements of meetings of all parties in the time of struggle were the scene of hot-tempered discussions, which for many Marxist workers were the first step towards the Movement of Adolf Hitler.

𝒯he SA man is always on duty. He does not stop being an SA man when he takes off the brown shirt, pursues his profession, or relaxes surrounded by his friends or his wife and children. On the contrary, in the political daily life nowadays the individual fighter has a task which is just as voluminous as it is responsible concerning ideological education and conviction of his comrades.

One saying of the Führer is: "I want the SA Mann to be the best politically educated National Socialist." In tough and hard detail work

Also "beauty of work" is a result of the SA fight.
As well as Marxism, the unscrupulous exploitation of the human worker was also almost completely eliminated. Parks offer to the working German people opportunities for sports and recreation in leisure time, where entertainment concerning ideology is not missing either.

the SA achieved this goal. Nowadays we see the success. However, it is a success which always has to be achieved again, in order not to lose it one day. The serious ideological opponent of the National Socialistic idea has defined the positions to break up the openly and hidden set foundation of the Führer's teachings. Rumors are being spread, enormous amounts of paper are being wasted, gossip is going around and is only right if we succeed in loosening the closed front of the German Nation or to educate them.

However, here you meet the unshaken resistance of the Truppen which not only carries the belief in Germany, taught to them according to the rule of their first Führer, but also are supposed to bring it to each German. The name of this Trupp, Sturmabteilung, describes it's spirit, a spirit which was never limited to defense, but to attack the position of the opponent, to never be discouraged by individual missed successes as long as there is an SA which had the final victory.

A bid will be evaluated higher the more sacrifices had to be brought to get there and the SA certainly has brought more than enough sacrifices for the union of the German Nation. So it is self-understood that today and in the future they are more than determined to keep this good, not for themselves, but for the sake of the Nation and their lives. And this battle of our day requires even new sacrifices like the one once fought for power. Even if the methods have changed, the final goal is the same.

The press frequently showed typical temporary figures with whom the unknown SA man had to fight the small battle of daily life. And even though carpers, complainers, and narrow-minded people, even though the politicizing clergy does not exactly need to characterize the type of person known to the public, many people are still carrying around with them the remains of liberalistic thinking, complaining about everything and forgetting that in the end they only support the enemies of the Reich. For just now the four-year plan brings with it certain limitations for each German in the Reich, revolutionizes the economy, and is taken aback at the same time by powerful actions under which the creation of German work and raw materials stands in the first place. All are supposed to, even have to, cooperate; only total devotion assures success. However, each involvement requires the internal readiness to harness all the energy, and this internal readiness guarantees and assures the backing of the Nation to the Leader who is responsible for the four-year plan, SA Obergruppenführer Hermann Göring. This has now become one of the present ideological tasks of the SA.

Even as soldiers at work, SA men stand with the first front.
A small group of fanatical fighters for Adolf Hitler, who look a little lost, once had been able to stand up to the Marxist superiority of the trade union terror in companies. Convinced by the National Socialistic idea of the SA, they nowadays form a big union. Former opponents have become comrades and co-fighters. The spirit of the SA won even here.

PRACTICAL INVOLVEMENT

Tomorrow will be Stew Sunday. The SA is peeling masses of potatoes the day before.
For a long time it has been spread around that the SA is ready for each task which may be
good for the Nation. In the SA nobody is too arrogant to peel potatoes for a stew; on the
contrary, for many of them this is a welcome change in the great variety of service, which here
receives the appropriate seasoning with music.

Right: "Umm, that smells good", the comrade at the portable field kitchen seems to think.
In field kitchens all over Germany on the so-called Stew Sundays where the whole
German Nation practices the practical socialism of action, the SA portable field kitchens are
ready to do their part, which for the SA is a thing of the heart. "Hunger revolts against the
SA", that's what foreign inflammatory papers wrote a few years ago! However, Germany
just laughs about it and goes to work respectfully making.........peas with a lot of bacon!

The nature of the SA today can be characterized by the fact that the political fighters against the old State have re-established a relation to all areas in life of the new State which is what we were fighting for and which they were building. Realizing that those who built the State were also responsible to further develop it in accordance with the plans and projects of the genius constructor Adolf Hitler, the new tasks of the SA resulted all by themselves.

The events of our day prove that the SA is going in the right direction. It unites the fighting will of political people with the ability to practically apply theoretical knowledge.

Catastrophe support duty, this is one of those tasks which the SA, like no other structure or organization, is responsible for in order to apply the sense of practical action socialism for the benefit of the people.

For example, there is protection from brush fires. Year by year many fires destroy valuable possessions. Carelessness, negligence, and frequently also malice, cause unmeasurable damages. The SA has made the fight against fires one of their essential tasks. At any time they are ready to act where they have to fight and extinguish fires.

Here and there hurricanes and cyclones destroy assets, houses, gardens and forests. In many cases, the SA Engineers are able to repair the damage in a very short time. When there is a power line destroyed by a storm, the SA communications engineer fixes it. We may want to mention the tidal waves which afflict the German coasts year after year. The worries and concerns which move the people are being decreased by the certainty that the SA is also on guard on the dikes and dams.

The SA has also taken on the task of saving endangered lives. In the last year many comrades were recognized by the Stabschef for their courageous actions. Among the effective health methods provided by the SA from its inner moral obligation is also the Winter Help Work, which is the people's social help support for the German Nation. Here the SA provides valuable services by applying their technical and propaganda methods, for example, field kitchens, music, parade music, homes, horses, etc. However, at the top of all those practical actions, is the education of the whole Nation by example and ideal. The SA exists for the people, both inside and outside of the community, and that is the most beautiful service that it can show to the Nation.

The Winter Help Work of the German Nation can rely on the cooperation of the SA.
Not only is the SA present when money is collected in the streets, but also in many individual and special actions. The
Sturmabteilungen provide room and resources for the WHW (Winter Help Work).

Fighting of brush fires.
An important task in the SA is involvement concerning catastrophes. Every year the German Nation suffers incredible damage caused by brush fires due to carelessness and negligence. Here the SA steps in, either by theoretical education, or by practical involvement in the case of fire. That the responsible authorities dealing with the prevention of damages closely cooperate with the SA shows how important this work is. All SA units are specifically headed by special SA Führers who deal with the prevention of catastrophes and damages and who we make responsible for taking care of these protection and prevention measures.

Here the storm has raged.
How many times has the SA been able to help in cases like this one. SA Engineers have learned during their service how to carefully remove the remains of a house. Piece by piece it is being removed and put aside. By doing this the men are in constant danger of being injured or even killed by falling posts and the remains of walls.

Right: A hurricane has destroyed the forest.
Many others are watching without doing anything. The SA Engineers are going to remove the damage using axes and saws. First the branches are removed from the trunks and neatly piled up, then the logs are cut, and finally the stumps dug or blown out. The Forstmeister (Forest Master) inspects the matter and generally has the opinion that without the SA they would have had a lot of inconveniences and paperwork, not to mention the high expenses of clearing the devastated forest.

As strange as it may sound, the cultural intentions of the SA have their origin in the daily political fight at the front of the past daily life. The numerous artists out of the National Socialistic rows, who already wore the brown shirt of the SA in the time of struggle, were also young revolutionaries in the fields of fine art and culture, who wanted to replace the foul and rotting with the healthy, the real, the divine and artistic sensitivity. But they cannot replace a thinking which recommended being "original by all means", with the insolent, the insane and the perverse as art.

And those who do not know anything of real, true art have paid high prices for scribblings applied by brushes on canvas of these would-be, low-level acrobats. Therefore, it is no surprise that the SA artists and their creations have especially found a great response in the House of German Art in Münich on the occasion of the Art Exhibition of the Third Reich. The result of the manual presentation of the soul and the internal sound of a talented individual is purity, popular clarity and visionary creativity. Therefore, the art of the men of the SA is a political art in the most superior and noble meaning, practiced by men who have the power to internally detach themselves the right distance, who forged the original material into really good form - in a way only a genuine artist can.

Every year the Cultural Circle of the SA applies a strong force all over Germany for this new cultural will. Men such as Josef Berchtold, Giesler, Franz, Moraller, Walter

SA artists in the State School of Bad Berka. In the Thüringia State School for Leadership and Politics, the Stabschef encouraged approximately 40 artists out of the SA ranks to be educated by Standartenführer Glöckler, Head of Department 4 of the Reichs Chamber of Creative Arts (now deceased). The students shown here, just some out of many, are busy completing a wall fresco.

Left: The right criticism.
Standartenführer Glöckler, himself a sculptor and creator of the SA Sports Badge and a Horst Wessel bust, during a critique of a plastic design. Here the critic is giving direction and encouragement to improve.

Right: "The Horseman of Valsgärde" is the name of this picture which was created by Wilhelm Petersen, an old SA man. Petersen, who also was very successful with his fine wood carvings, was authorized by Reichsleiter Rosenberg to teach art interpretation of past German history in schools.

"Ours – the future!"
The SA celebrations also had their own style. This came from the time of struggle, and was formed, hardened and refined and nowadays is of artistic and political value in the front of daily life.

God is with the strong ones.
Georg Sluyterman von Langewede, a German etcher and wood carver, received his best artistic motive as an SA man long before taking over power. His works show the bitter defiance of the so-called "coal pot", which strongly fought for the Ruhr District against alien occupation, slavery and artistic rape – political art in its highest completion.

Heitmüller, Klähn, Hanns Schaudinn, Hans Zöberlein, Oskar Glöckler, Gerhard Schumann, Otto Paust, Dr. Zeitler, Goetz Otto Stoffregen, Hans Peter Hermel, the Führer of the Cultural Circle of the SA Willi Körbel, Herbert Böhme, Bernd Lembeck, Dietrich Loder, Heinrich Anacker, Waldemar Glaser, Kurt Massmann, Dr. Hans Volz, Rudolf v. Elmayer-Bestenbrugg, Herbert Menzel, Erich Lauer,

God gave a comrade to each fighter.
These words written by Herybert Menzels could be written underneath the glass picture of Professor Schwartzkopf, which is exquisitely impressive concerning its fine beauty of colors and unusual presentation of heroes. The Sturm comrade takes the banner out of the hand of the fallen fighter in order to carry it to victory.

Poetry from the people.
The same way the SA got their power for fighting and the ability to conquer Germany for the whole Nation, so the poets are in the middle of the people, from whom they receive the blessed order to make a poem of life and to create it purely and valuably. Not only for the people's sake, not just for fine art's sake, have they struggled with the problem to force the material into form by their art. Here Herbert Böhme can be seen talking to workers of the Reichsbahn.

Helmuth Hansen, within the Cultural Circle of the SA, dedicate all their creations to expressing the lifestyle of this new art, which is carried by the cultural will of the SA to all areas: radio, music, theater, press, poetry, literature, etc. Many of them have become an unchangeable program among the people, and not only in Germany. Often the men from the SA, of whose creations we show only a very small section, and who themselves could fill whole halls in the House of German Art, cross the border and speak to foreign comrades with whom they are related by blood and language, concerning intellectual thoughts of the Third Reich

An SA poet is reading.
When one SA poet, for example out of the Cultural Circle, is reading, then this is the guarantee for contemporary pureness of style in the tone, content and the whole performance. At the same time, it is a certainty of sold out houses, without which any cultural performance directed to the whole Nation, and not addressed to the individual parts, would be senseless. Frequently the poets of the Cultural Circle are invited abroad in order to give a picture of the contemporary intellectual thought and its creators to the German national groups.

Right: "March Block Dürer".
So-called ones in a series of SA artists, they themselves of the Movement, in Nuremberg, well-earned and through the Adolf Hitler Free Resort days, filled with wonderful experiences and artistic activities, worn out and spent. They were marching, however not under the motto "Obligatory obedience - Healthy motif!". Instead of backpacks they carried easels, instead of bread bags they carried palettes, brushes and canvases, and sometimes the march block was all in, but by watercolors, oils, tripods and horizons.

The word and the gesture.
In all fields the cultural willingness and support of the SA can be noted. The art of dominating words and gestures in order to express certain topics is mastered by many amateur plays. What could be closer than the material relationships of the front soldiership, such as "The Endless Road! (By Sigmund Graff and Carl Ernst Hintze.)

about their own work - as political soldiers!

The SA ceremonies, their celebration hours, poetry events, and music performances are all spent by our great fighting community whose artists are not only the SA's but also Germany's best ones, who proudly wear the brown shirts and the armbands, who have fought and suffered with us (Professor Hans Schwarz had to pay with his life for being convinced politically and artistically) who, impregnated by their mission to artistically explain our life, always confessed, "We are SA men"!

The Cultural Circle of the SA with Dr. Goebbels.
On the occasion of a work conference in Berlin, the Cultural Circle of the SA, headed by Sturmbannführer Hermel, is received by the Reichsminister for Peoples Education and Propaganda, Dr. Goebbels.

PHYSICAL EXERCISES AND MILITARY SPORTS OF THE SA

THE VISIBLE EXPRESSION OF SA SERVICE FOR THE NATION IS MEETING THE REQUIREMENTS OF THE SA SPORTS BADGE. Almost one and half million Germans already have this badge, which now has to be earned every year.

The SA Sports Badge Office in the SA High Command is busy processing the approximately 4,000 petitions which they receive and get ready for shipment daily. Each German comrade who is Aryan and has never been convicted of a felony can receive this badge, which is visible official proof of physical ability and military sports capability. If he is a "semi-skilled" outsider, he has to report to an outdoor sports work community where he will be trained, pass the test, and then receive the badge and the holder's certificate from his tester and instructor. There are approximately 5,500 testers (who in the future, as well as the 35,000 holders of the instructor certificate, have to go through the SA schools). He gives a result card to the responsible SA Sports Badge Office of the Gruppe, the other stays with the Sports Badge Office in the SA High Command. The issue is registered the same moment the oblong is stamped, "In the name of the Führer-Lutze". By using a helpful perforation procedure, the statistical evaluation on the cards can be evaluated in the shortest time. These result cards are registered in a huge central registration index according to the official community directory for the German Nation and their District. The SA Sports Badge does not require any maximum performance, but is for the masses with average results, specifically concerning military sports. All military sports and the SA tournaments are based on a logical development of natural physical exercises, also the movements — walking, running, tumbling, obstacle racing — and only in systematical

Military sports become popular sports.
True to the Führer's decree of March 18, 1937, which became valid January 1, 1938, the holders of the SA Sports Badge have to be retrained every year. However, at the same time their performance book becomes a diploma. By this a big step has been taken to maintain physical ability through military sports. The newly created Main Headquarters of the NS Kampfspiele (Combat Competitions) in Berlin will continue planned military sports for the masses. However, systematic training is necessary to take obstacles like these as a team. It is not important how quickly only one or the other will overcome it, but all.

Shot!
In team tournaments, swimming specifically plays an important role. Here the starter's pistol was fired and the men, equipped with uniforms, boots and knapsacks, plunged into the water. Mere seconds determined the victory of this team.

Done!
Totally exhausted and still completely out of breath, the winner climbs the edge of the pool. Even though the first meters seem to be easy, the last few meters, however, take their toll due to the uniform soaked by water, the knapsack and the boots. The more difficult the circumstances, the more successful the test for the fighting involvement in an emergency.

PHYSICAL EXERCISES AND MILITARY SPORTS OF THE SA

Only for people with no fear of heights. The SA, always being ready to act, has been hardened by their actions. However, in order to be useful, it requires appropriate physical preparation, as climbing steep walls like here. The south wall of the middle Gans in the Sächsischen rocky mountains is not for amateurs.

Goal!
Wearing a uniform while running is quite a hindrance. The same for wearing a gas mask! On the occasion of an SA Brigade sports event in Berlin, this 4 x 100 meter run of the Standarte requires a lot of effort concerning heart and lungs of the competitors. And in the heat!

Between heaven and earth.
The SA physical exercises not only train the human being to physical ability, persistence and tenacity, but also primarily in courage and self-confidence. As here this man is hanging on a rope between the first and second floors as exercise. He has self-confidence and knows what his body can do.

We must pass them....
With a lot of work, Sturme and Standartes have built their own arenas, many hours and free Sundays were spent doing so; obstacles were built, either wire obstacles, log obstacles, ditches, crawling ways, wooden walls, etc. Here they exercise their bodies without hesitating. In team tournaments to strengthen their comradeship, they all have to pass. Spectators and participants are excited in the same way to see if they can pass despite the equipment they carry – and the ditch is very deep.

Hang in there!
Marches where they carry equipment are the preferred area for the German who relentlessly marches in the field. Just consider the events of the last maneuvers. That's why the marches where they carry equipment have an important part in physical exercises, endurance – with a cheerful song and the rhythm of the old fighting melodies, they are heading to the goal. That is why it is no coincidence that one SA formation (Brigade 35 Leipzig) became the German champion.

PHYSICAL EXERCISES AND MILITARY SPORTS OF THE SA

Almost.
Yes, he almost succeeded and then he would not h
to carry such a sour face. Only one more foo
and he would not have fallen down
(which he is about to do). Bu
carrying several knapsa
there is nothing y
can do to s

According to temperament.
Competition also means the com-
petitor's shout, which has settled
some victories of the so-called
"famous centimeter", "hand-
shake" or "width of chest".
Depending on the tempera-
ment of the men at that
time, from a smile up to
blazing enthusiasm, they go
on participating professionally.

Boys, pull hard!
Tug-of-war can get
spectators and par-
ticipants to boil, espe-
cially if the thick rope
does not give way even a
slight space, to give way
by one centimeter, so that
this one or the other one
wins. There really is an art to
shouting, to holding and to
pulling; however, it is always
fun!

training of the men, with or without equipment, during contests and tournaments (loosening of the muscles, tendons, enlarging of the lungs, etc.) man is made tough for endurance. In addition, there is the technical education. We must bear in mind, that in the first place in the assumed power structure, the words "sports and physical exercises" as military sports are an unknown concept in their lives. Yet on it goes constantly from success to success. The NS tournaments in 1937 on the occasion of the Reichs Party Day showed the big successful prelude for the command: Training of the Nation - the so-called "synthesis of spirit and body", gradually real-

ized by the SA. Combat sports were added to the real military sports, in which cheerfulness and humor are not missing. Those who so far have practiced little or no sports at all start with the competitions in order to loosen up again. Just go to one of the SA arenas and see how the General Director participates in the tug-of-war against his packing master. Generally this is the secret of each success: to learn during the game! The struggle as a basic element increases the successes from small to large performances.

Gruppenführer Wilhelm Kleinmann
stellv. Generaldirektor der Dt. Reichsbahn
(Acting General Director of the Reichs Railways)

Gruppenführer Christian Mergenthaler
Württemb. Ministerpräsident
(Minister President of Württemburg)

Gruppenführer Georg Oberdieck
Beisitzer im Volksgerichtshof
(Member of the People's Court)

Obergruppenführer Wilhelm Weiss
Hauptschriftleiter des "V. B."
(Chief Editor of the VB)

TO BE AN SA MAN MEANS TO HAVE DEDI-
CATED HIS LIFE TO THE SIGN WHICH IS
THE SYMBOL OF LOYALTY AND PERSIST-
ENCE FOR THE GERMAN FOR ALL TIMES.
THE MEN WHO NOWADAYS WORK, FOR
EXAMPLE, AS AN SA FÜHRER IN STATE
AUTHORITY AND WORK IN THE PARTY FOR
THE PEOPLE'S SAKE, WAS STANDING NEXT
TO US WHILE FIGHTING FOR GERMANY,
NEXT TO YOU AND ME AND BEING REALLY
GOOD COMRADES TO US. THEY CARRIED
THE BANNER AND WON JOBS AND BREAD
FOR THE NATION BY FIGHTING. THEN THE
FÜHRER CALLED THEM IN FOR NEW WORK.
AS STORM SOLDIERS THEY CONTINUED TO
WORK IN THE GROWING RECONSTRUC-
TION BUT THEY WILL ALWAYS BE WHAT
THEY ALWAYS WERE DURING THE FIGHT
FOR THE REICH, SA COMRADES!

Gruppenführer Hanns Oberlindober
Reichskriegsopferführer (Reichs War Sacrifice Leader)(Editor's
note: for wounded and relatives of war killed)

Obergruppenführer Hermann Kriebel
Generalkonsul in Schanghai
(General Consul in Shanghai)

The basic attitude of the SA is military. Its task
has to take this nature into account: work not only in
the military sense, but also the physical and mental
military training of the people based on the National
Socialistic ideology.

To be an SA man means to work as a political
soldier for the Führer and the Nation in the
service of Adolf Hitler.

The German is not ennobled by birth, but by the
best fulfillment of his duties for country and Nation
and absolute loyalty to our great Führer, Adolf Hitler!

In the task in front of me I see unlimited possibilities to bring the socialism of action in the SA spirit to
the population at Rhein and Ruhr.

Forever the SA and Germany are inseparable terms.

Obergruppenführer Fritz Reinhard
Staatssekretär im Reichsfinanzministerium
(State Secretary at the Reichs Finance Ministry)

Gruppenführer Herzog von Coburg

Gruppenführer Ludwig Uhland
Landesgruppenführer Rheinland des NLB.
(District Gruppe Leader Rheinland of the NLB)

Gruppenführer Wilh. Frhr. v. Schorlemer
Reichssportführung
(Reichs Sports Director)

Obergruppenführer Kurt v. Ulrich
Oberpräsident der Provinz Sachsen
(First President of the Province Sachsen)

Obergruppenführer Hans-Georg Hofmann
Staatssekr. b. Reichsstatthalter in Bayern
(State Secretary and Reichs Governor in Bavaria)

Obergruppenführer Fritz Sauckel
Reichsstatthalter Thüringen
(Reichs Governor of Thuringen)

Each SA man has the obligation and responsibility, especially each SA Führer, no matter which position he is in, to contribute by his life and his actions to make the SA spirit the general thinking and property of the whole German Nation.

Only in this way will he always be ever ready to assist our Führer in his extremely difficult task.

In old times fighting was nicer; now the mission of the SA is more important and the leadership more difficult!

Obergruppenführer Julius Streicher
Gauleiter Franken
(District Leader of Franken)

Obergruppenführer Manfred v. Killinger
Generalkonsul in San Francisco
(General Consul in San Francisco)

My involvement in the SA is determined by the tasks for the Nation and the Führer. As already mentioned in the so-called "Obligation of the SA Man" (the SA bible) when I was SA Führer of the Gruppe Bavaria in the year 1931, the SA's first task was to protect against enemy forces in the time of struggle. So as they once conquered the streets for the liberation of Germany from the red danger, they nowadays watch the political will of the Movement so that the new Reich remains unharmed by the forces of disintegration.

The SA is the serving force of the National Socialistic Movement; it is the expression of the idealistic and selfless thinking of the German mind, and for this reason is permanent.

Right is what is good for our people, wrong is what damages them. To act accordingly, without fear and persistently, is the task of the SA.

Obergruppenführer Wilhelm Brückner
Chefadjutant des Führers
(Chief Adjutant of the Führer)

Gruppenführer Erich Hasse
Landrat Niederelbe
(District Administrator Niederelbe)

Obergruppenführer Josef Wagner
Gauleiter und Oberpräsident von Schlesien
(District Leader and First President of Schlesien)

Gruppenführer Alfred Meyer
Reichsstatthalter Schaumburg-Lippe
(Reichs Governor Schaumburg-Lippe)

Gruppenführer Dr. Otto Wagener

Gruppenführer Ludwig SiebertBayer.
Ministerpräsident
(Bavarian Minister President)

Obergruppenführer Hans Frank
Reichsminister
(Reichs Minister)

Gruppenführer Rudolf Schmeer
Hauptdienstleiter der NSDAP.
(Senior Service Leader of the NSDAP)

Gruppenführer Julius Lippert
Stadtpräsident von Berlin
(City President of Berlin)

The SA is the secure, never-stopping engine which constantly drives the German men to the highest National Socialistic virtues: courage and discipline, loyalty and camaraderie, ready to act for the Führer and the Nation.

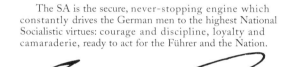

I was closely related to the SA concerning the fighting for power. Nothing has changed after taking over power, and nothing will ever change.

Whoever belongs to the SA has given his life to Germany. He cannot stay out of the fight in order to completely eliminate the Jewish parasites. This parasite has the name "capitalistic economical system". Its guardians are the free masons and their friends. The fight against them will always be a real task for the SA.

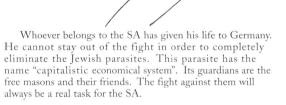

The Reich's capital will always march in unison with the SA and always remember the merits of the SA when conquering Berlin.

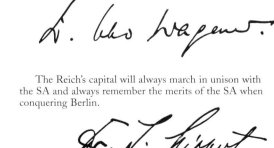

We the SA Führers who were assigned leading positions in the State, never want to forget that without the loyalty of the SA men we never would have had these positions.

Gruppenführer Carl Röver
Reichsstatthalter Oldenburg
(Reichs Governor Oldenburg)

Obergruppenführer Josef Bürckel
Reichskommissar der Saarpfalz
(Reichs Commissioner of Saarpfalz)

Gruppenführer Franz v. Pfeffer
Regierungspräsident Wiesbaden
(Governmental President Wiesbaden)

Gruppenführer Heinz Späing
Landrat in Langensalza
(District Administrator in Langensalza)

Gruppenführer Willy Marschler
Thüring. Ministerpräsident
(Minister President of Thüringen)

Obergruppenführer Dr. Gerhard Wagner
Reichsärzteführer
(Reichs Physician Leader)

Obergruppenführer Robert Ley
Reichsorganisationsleiter
(Reichs Organization Leader)

Obergruppenführer Josef Terboven
Gauleiter u. Oberpräsident in Essen
(District Leader and First President in Essen)

Obergruppenführer Frz. Xaver Schwarz
Reichsschatzmeister der NSDAP.
(Reichs Treasurer of the NSDAP)

As an old SA man I will always defend the necessity of the SA. It is necessary as long as the fight for Germany goes on.

The SA is the carrier of the "always ready to fight" tradition of the National Socialistic Party.

This fighting spirit was transmitted to new tasks.

The SA man uses all of his pride and power to fulfill the tasks given to him by the State and District Administration of the National Socialistic Reich with proud SA spirt and as always, serves the Führer and the German Nation with devotion and irresistible loyalty, despite the individual work of the State apparatus.

It is the task and obligation of the SA to march in the first front regarding health questions, popular politics, race culture and old fighting spirit - as an example for the whole German Nation.

The SA physicians have to perform an especially important and responsible education work.

Vigilance, willingness to fight, and selfless involvement is the permanent creed of the SA.

SA spirit is loyalty, courage to sacrifice, and fulfillment of obligations.

Following these ideals the SA man successfully fought in Germany's roughest times and the belief in these ideals nowadays gives him the energy to master and complete each task given to him by the National Socialistic State.

Gruppenführer Franz Schwede-Coburg
Gauleiter u. Oberpräsident von Pommern
(District Leader and First President of Pommerania)

Obergruppenführer Bernhard Rust
Reichsmin. f. Wissensch., Erz. u. Volksbildg.
(Reichs Minister for Science and Education)

Gruppenführer Arthur Hess
Reichsinnungsmeister
(Reichs Guild Master)

Obergruppenführer Franz v. Epp
Reichsstatthalter in Bayern
(Reichs Governor in Bavaria)

Obergruppenführer Adolf Wagner
Gauleiter München-Oberbayern
(District Leader of München and Upper Bavaria)

Obergruppenführer Wilhelm Jahn
Polizeipräsident von Halle
(Police President in Halle)

Obergruppenführer F. K. Florian
Gauleiter in Düsseldorf
(District Leader in Düsseldorf)

The hardest task of our time is the creation of the true community. It can, in the best meaning, only exist in equal conviction and voluntary dedication. However, nowhere were these conditions fulfilled as in the SA; nowhere like here can Socialists and Nationalists became real comrades; nowhere like here even the life of the poorest had a new meaning and he himself the consciousness of the whole country. The spirit which resulted out of this therefore is the most valuable good. To maintain, care for and propagate it is still the best service for the work of the Führer.

Marxer

The SA successfully resolved its former task to cause a breakthrough to the thinking of the Führer. Today it has become our destiny to give this thought to the whole German Nation as the right of existence. The individual as well as the Nation may be convinced by using words; however, examples are more effective.

As an SA Führer in State services, I see my most noble task in the complete penetration of the official system with National Socialistic thinking, in the education of being ready for action and to be willing to sacrifice, in the meaning of the old fighting troop of the Führer.

Jahn

Obergruppenführer Baldur v. Schirach
Reichsjugendführer
(Reichs Youth Leader)

Obergruppenführer Hinrich Lohse
Gauleiter in Schleswig-Holstein

With pride the front soldier carries his wounds and his badges! With no lesser pride the SA man is wearing his wounds and the badges of the NSDAP received while fighting for Germany! However, only his fight brought meaning and completeness to the Big War in the Third Reich.

Otto Wagner.

The same way we could help the Führer as storm-proven fighters and SA men to conquer the Reich for the National Socialism, today we have to see our most noble tasks and obligations filled by the old SA spirit in order to maintain it for him forever!

Willy Liebel

Obergruppenführer Hanns Kerrl
Reichsminister f. kirchliche Angelegenheiten
(Reichs Minister For Church Affairs)

Gruppenführer Otto Marxer

Gruppenführer Willy Liebel
Oberbürgermeister der Stadt Nuremberg
(Mayor of the City of Nuremberg)

Gruppenführer Prinz August Wilhelm

Gruppenführer Arthur Rakobrandt
Landesgruppenführer VII des RLB
(District Gruppe Leader VII of the RLB)

Gruppenführer Graf Helldorf
Polizeipräsident von Berlin
(Police President of Berlin)

Obergruppenführer Martin Mutschmann
Reichsstatthalter in Sachsen
(Reichs Governor in Sachsen)

Obergruppenführer Rudolf Jordan
Gauleiter von Magdeburg–Anhalt
(District Leader of Magdeburg–Anhalt)

Gruppenführer Hocheisen

Obergruppenführer Franz Seldte
Reichsarbeitsminister
(Reichs Labor Minister)

Gruppenführer Kurt Lasch

Gruppenführer Fritz Todt
Generalinspekt. f. d. deutsche Strassenwesen
(General Inspector for German Road Construction)

The SA sees their most dutiful task in the ability to fight in the first line as the so-called "Socialists of Action"!
SA spirit created the new State. In the spirit of the old SA we will defend and maintain it.

I see the SA man as the most loyal comrade in the political as well as life struggle. So his task will be in the German people's community of the National Socialistic State for all time.

Always the SA man had his place in the past where the hardest and truest struggle was. Also in the future his place is the same and in this place he is supposed to be what he always was, the man of hard action.

The task of the Reich Air Protection Union (RLB) is to give to our people their moral power and energy to withstand any enemy attack to the home country successfully.
    This task can only be fulfilled when the National Socialistic ideology becomes common knowledge and remains the guideline of our actions! The old fighting spirit of the SA has to be in each individual of our officials if we want to educate the whole Nation to cooperate in air protection, and so in the defense of the country.
    However, this is our goal!

The courageous spirt of the SA man from the time of struggle also had to be in the German engineer; then his buildings will become memorials of our time.

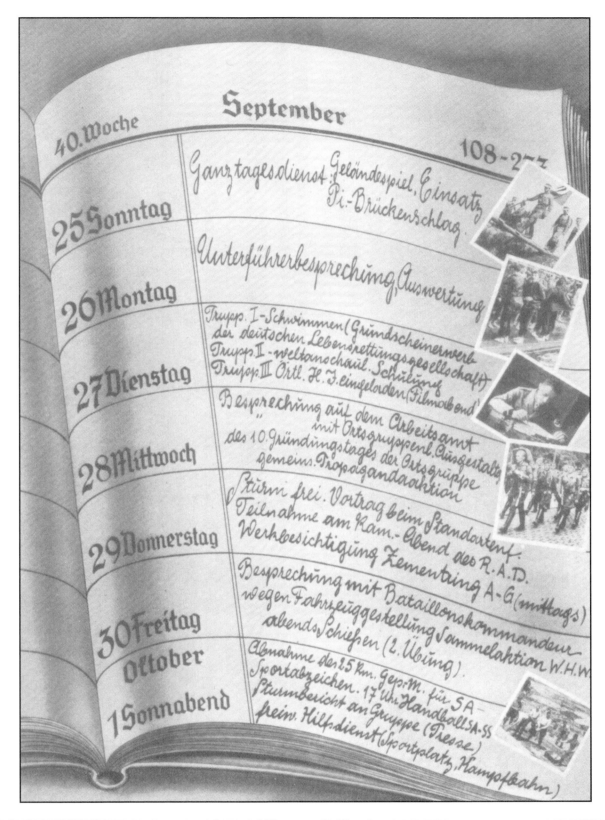

25 Sunday
Full day's work: Help with cross-country games
Engineer bridge building

26 Monday
Unterführer conference, Evaluation

27 Tuesday
Trupp. I - Swimming (Basic public certification of
the German Lifesaving Society)
Trupp. II - Philosophy indoctrination
Trupp. III - Local HJ Offload (film night)

28 Wednesday
Conference with the Labor Office with the Ortsgruppenführer
on the status of the 10 Foundation Days of the Ortsgruppe
Community Propaganda Action.

29 Thursday
Sturm free lecture by the Standartenführer.
Attend the camaraderie night of the R.A.D.
Work inspection Cement Circle Corporation (Noon)

30 Friday
Conference with battalion commander for vehicle call-up for fund
raising campaign for WHW.
Night shooting match (2 practice).

October
1 Saturday
Inspection for the 25 km. pack-march for the
SA-Sports Badge. 5:00 p.m. handball SA-SS
Sturm report on the Gruppe (Press)
Volunteer Help Service (Sports field, competition course)

MEMORIALS OF THE SA

"In appreciation of the SA merits during the time of struggle."
In all Districts of the Reich in the last few years, streets and places were renamed "Street of the SA" or "Place of the SA". Those areas, cities and towns in which the toughest battles took place were the first ones that expressed their appreciation for the political soldiers of the Führer in this way.

It was like this in many villages and towns. The men in brown shirts conquered the streets for the German people, in which the Bolshevik mob believed they had the sole right. So it is more than right that these German streets are also renamed by the system which cleaned these streets of all enemies of the Nation as assault troops.

Honor and recognition by others are symbols accompanying success, whether it is bouquets of flowers or shadow-casting trees along both sides of the road through which the fighting troops or an individual marches. In the same way we are supposed to be evaluated; because determination and willingness to act do not take the way which promises the most beauty, but the one which best leads to the goal. Only lack of action and internal emptiness need other people's opinion as motivation, only they look in irrelevant distance points and theirs exists - and they lose their direc-

In Hamburg a simple but impressive memorial was created in appreciation of the murdered of the Movement. In some towns the struggle for power was so hard, required so much involvement and willingness to sacrifice; however, it was the worst in the old city of Hansa. The names of the fighters who gave their best and their life for the Führer can be read on the sacrificial bowl, which is in the center of the memorial. Not in words is the gratitude, but in the action and the service of the German people which was the highest for them.

The Movement triumphed in this sign. This eagle is on the roof of the "Standarte" of the Führer in the "Deutscher Hof" in the city of the Reichs Party Days, created by an SA man.

"Comrades shot by the Red Front and Reaction...."
Across from the Horst Wessel House in what used to be the center of the Berlin KPD, the Karl Leibknecht House, you can see the enormous stone memorial in the east of the Reich capital, in which there are the names of those who fell in the center of Berlin. The names are headed by Horst Wessel's, whose assassination began the final part of the decisive conflict of the SA with the Berlin Bolshevik, in which they were finally destroyed.

tion over it. The first successes are always the hardest ones, especially those pursued away from the public. However, appreciation is for the future. Total dedication to an idea, idealism and sacrifices can hardly be completely expressed in stone and metal. They are invisible to most people. It is the same way with the SA victories for which they fought the hardest. Only very few know about these stations where comrades, dock workers, middle class sons and farmers did much more than ever before. They remain unknown as individuals. However, all of them helped the Führer's ideas take life and shape in millions of German people, when their own ego was in the background behind their goal. If a name was mentioned, it was not a man's name, but a Trupp's name, and it became the term for idealistic fighting in the life of the Nation. The individual political soldier never claimed gratitude and appreciation and did not even expect it. When today the SA receives appreciation, when we find memorials in towns and villages and in streets and places of the German Reich, such as the Horst-Wessel-Haus in Berlin, the man in the brown shirt considers this a memorial to those who made major sacrifices and whose blood welded together the SA fighting union into an indestructible unit.

The SA Memorial in Magdeburg.
The way of the SA, which was the way of the National Socialistic Movement, is and will always be symbolized in the memorial constructed by the SA Gruppe Mitte for their murdered men. The flight of the German eagle symbolizes the advancing revolutionary power of the idea, whose most active carriers are the men in brown shirts who, fulfilled by the unshakeable belief in their ideology, brought this belief to the whole German Nation and conquered the hearts for the Führer and his Reich.

*D*oubts and objections are the enemy of every new lesson. When the National Socialistic ideology of life intruded into the picture of German life, it formed a political army with their best fighters used for protection of their meetings and demonstrations, the SA. Here we can reject conflicting opinions and interpretations and the objection that today numerous divisions marching side by side would disturb and destroy the Party and its positive political work. The purpose, tasks and changing requirements of our struggle have resulted in the Party structures out of the big SA reservoir.

If we go back a few pages in the book of time, in the beginning was the Party and the SA, their strong arm feared by the opponents. Soldiers, workers, farmers and youth were marching in disciplined units who, secretly disguised, were active for the first time under the protection of the SA. This later created a platform for the big youth organization, the HJ. Very soon the lining up of special formations within the SA proved absolutely necessary. So the Führer created, for example, the *SS* squadron for special purposes. Efficient SA men were the basis for it. The growing tasks and unchangeable signs of the fight against the system then resulted in the independence of these special formations. In this way the former Motor-SA became today's NSKK, the first "flight sturmes" resulted in the National Socialist Flight Korps, the NSFK. Let us recall that many political leaders, Kreis and Ortsgruppenleiters, who advise and guide the organization of the Party today, were SA men and SA Führers during the time of struggle, in order to realize that the strong impulses which came from the SA were transferred to all branches of the independent work of all Party structures. In recent times, this was proven by the formation of work groups which, in close cooperation with the SA, were supposed to represent the correct attitude in factories and plants, which the SA today, like yesterday, lives as an example. The ways and matters of today's political fight have changed. The Party structures fulfill their tasks according to their own laws and responsibilities. Whoever used to march in the columns, however, will always feel that they have a little bit of this attitude and spirit in them which we call the SA spirit.

Günther Curth first joins the HJ.....
The German way of life begins in the Hitler Youth,
which prepares the boy for his way in the community
of his people, who he has to serve all of his life.

In the time of struggle, the educational involvement first began with the youth. The martyrs of the HJ are the saints of the first youthful community, whose loyalty and belief never fell behind that of the best old people. The word "education" is not needed in order to make clear that the old HJ was the first haven of political instruction in the National Socialist Movement. In the idealistic generation of the war internally, the total thought of the Movement was fulfilled. This is the HJ's tradition, which in addition to home and school, has a purpose in the political education of the German youth. Thanks to this task, the Hitler Youth is in a position to set the Party's evaluation rules as a fine mesh colander between youth and reality for each individual who wants to grow into responsibility.

By taking the 18-year-old Hitler Youth into the SA, the consciously political influence on the young people begins. The SA takes over the education process and effectively applies their valuable teaching and education methods for a temporary period concerning political education and character forming of the young fighters.

....and then the SA.
Here begins his ideological and political
education, and the physical training
teaches him hard lessons.

entered civilian life without internal or external obligation as the fruits of his service. Here the fighting organizations of the Party jump in. The SA, SS and NSKK involve the returning soldier in a new area of obligations, continues according to content and meaning the educational work of the Arbeitsdienst and military in a new work area, matching youthful thirst for action, intended for a new human being who successfully passed through the Arbeitsdienst and the armed forces.

It is to say that especially the SA, their tradition and their modern actions have become the center of fit soldiers. They want to form the political soldier into a carrier of arms. The political soldier is the new type of human being who, beyond individualism, is collectively the basic element of the new German State ideal.

The Führer himself has determined the educational value of the young human being for all time: "The boy, he will join the Jungvolk, and as a young man he will join the Hitler Youth, and the youths of the Hitler Youth will join the SA, the SS and all the other groups.

From the work force Günther Curth joins the Armed Forces
For two years he has been trained with weapons, learned to obey, and to fit in at the great training school of the Nation, which from now on each German, without exception, has to go through. The Army makes him a soldier, a fighter, using weapons which are supposed to be a strong protection for the country and the people.

Work and military service continue the young people's education by using other means and ways. Today everybody realizes that work and military service are important steps on the way to maturity and personality. The experiences of five years illustrate that the way is correct. The youth, the future of the Nation, got used to the new education. Everybody still has to make sacrifices. There is no more room for exception and privileges in the schools of the coming generations.

The educational work of the Hitler Youth, the Arbeitsdienst (work service), and the Army would only raise for itself little efficiency concerning the educational evidences of the pre-war Army if the soldier dismissed from the services

Work ennobles!
The last station prior to the military service is the Work Service which teaches the young people to recognize the value of manual work.

Back in the SA.
Two years have passed. Günther Curth marches again as a political soldier. The education is finished. The way into life begins. They are SA men for life.

The SA man and SS man one day will join the Arbeitsdienst and from there the Army. Then the people's soldier will return to the organization of the Movement of the Party in the SA and SS, and never again will our people be as down as they used to be."

The individual destiny of one comrade, SA man Günther Curth of Berlin, whose brother Udo fell for the new Reich, here in these pictures shows the way of life of all young Germans.

Natural performance of duty, which both Mann and leader equally performed as political soldiers of Adolf Hitler, characterizes the SA's involvement in work, not records. If we now mention some figures in this area, it is for no other purpose than to show to the public the achievements of men, achievements of which nobody speaks. These deeds, however, have meaning for everybody and express the internal attitude of the organization which performed them as examples of selfless devotion to an idea, which nowadays as yesterday, demanded everybody's sacrifices without giving anything back except an awareness of having done his duty to the Führer. We may not mention the names of any men or units; as the man and his Trupp fall into the background behind everybody's interests, which we all serve. The SA fighting involvement has nothing to do with the fact of creating records, but is for the creation of a new German human being. This requires a degree of work, which is done the same way by the Sturmsoldaten (storm soldiers) in the so-called coalfield, just as those men on the coasts who work as dock hands, for example, the timber worker or farmer of the highlands through their own spirit and action, the officials from the heart of the Reich, or the miners out of the Oberschlesischen (Upper Silesian) coalfield. They altogether helped conquer and build up the new State and they all continue working on its completion, each in his place where the Führer put him.

- In 1937, for example, one Sturm acted six times in catastrophe cases. Among those were two forest fires, a flood, two property-damaging farm fires, and a hail storm.

- Men out of the same unit saved seven lives from drowning in the year 1937.

- During a collection for the Winter Help Work, an SA Rottenführer sold 1,217 badges.

- On his way to his Sturm assembly, a Truppführer has to go 20 kilometers each way. Being on duty twice a week he goes approximately 4,300 kilometers a year by bicycle from his flat to the local Sturm, no matter what kind of weather.

- On the occasion of a collection of trash and junk 70,000 men were on duty in one city of the Reich on a single Sunday.

- The number of SA Sports Badges handed out increased from 155,269 in the year 1934 to 424,896 in the following year, and reached 442,349 in the year 1936, and today there are approximately 1.5 million holders of the SA Sports Badge in the Reich.

- In order to build streets in one war sacrifice housing area, the men of one Trupp put in 500 hours of labor without getting paid, another Sturm put in 4,000 hours labor to build an SA sports arena.

- Out of a Sturm of 133 men, 131 have the SA Sports Badge, 102 the Certificate of the German Society to Save Human Lives.

- One SA Standarte of 3,000 men have the same number of comrades in the SA Sports Badge community.

- Out of an SA Reserve Sturm of 146 men, 120 men received the SA Sports Badge, among these 30 were over 50 years old, and two were over 60 years old.

- In the "Hilfswerk Camp" Camp Lockstedter, whose purpose is to train skilled workers, more than 1,000 former unskilled workers received their journeyman certificates.

- By the ""Thanks Offering of the Nation" the men of one Sturm, consisting mainly of manual workers, distinguished themselves by collecting no less than 850 marks through the efforts of 114 men.

These figures are examples out of the existing statistics. They could be supplemented in many ways. However, this seems unnecessary as already the above numbers are proof enough to show everybody that the SA spirit is alive and always ready to sacrifice, which they do.

𝒯here is no other picture presentation of the changing times in Germany which so clearly presents the old and the new Germany like pictures of the Karl Leibknecht House and the Horst Wessel House. The first name already characterizes the chaos and the fall, and the other is the symbol of the new re-strengthened, independent Reich. And this is also the way the houses look. The first one was dirty, bloody, with glaring transparencies that mark the Red headquarters, mark the spot in which Jews

Fight the Red Berlin.
A group of members of Sturm 1 at the Reichs capital city, which had the name "Sturm 1, Alexander". To the very right, Horst Wessel, whose name, life and assassination became a symbol, even beyond the borders of his home, for the struggle of the Sturmabteilungen of Adolf Hitler for a new Reich.

Horst Wessel was dead but his spirit continued to live on in the hearts and fists of his comrades.
On February 23, 1930 the Berlin Sturmführer who had created the song of the National Socialist Revolution died as the result of an assault by the Communist Ali Höhler. His co-fighters carried the coffin from the funeral home in the Jüdenstrasse to the car. The Bolshevik underworld did not even give any rest to the dead. Cursing and thrown rocks accompanied the procession. A few years later however, the prophetic words of Horst Wessel were fulfilled, Hitler's flags were flying in all streets, the time of slavery was over.

HORST WESSEL

IN IHREM GEIST VORWÄRTS IM KAMPF

GEGEN KRIEGSGEFAHR. FASCHISMUS. HUNGER

UND FROST. FÜR ARBEIT. BROT

U. FREIHEIT

HORST WESSEL

By this time Moscow's game in the Reich was over.
The SA march on January 22, 1933 at the Vülowplatz in front of the Karl Liebknecht House brought the breakdown of the Jewish Bolshevik terror in Berlin. It was a blow which the Communists were not able to get over. With the fall of the center the clean-up work started, which was extraordinarily and successfully performed within a very short time.

The Karl Liebknecht House became the Horst Wessel House, which nowadays is the service center of the SA Gruppe Berlin-Brandenburg.
The legacy of the pioneer and assassinated hero Horst Wessel could not have been fulfilled any better than by having the ideas he had been fighting for and gave his life for brought to victory, and as an external symbol, the house in which the plan for elimination was created was named for him. Completely rebuilt, simple, clean and clear in its internal and external design, today the Horst Wessel House has become a landmark of the National Socialistic Berlin.

came up with the brutal murder plan to assassinate Horst Wessel. Hideouts, secret rooms and a basement equipped with heavy metal doors showed that this house used to serve the Revolution.

Today the Horst Wessel House is simple and clean. Structural adjustments made to the place which used to be one of Berlin's blemishes, make it a nice place today. SA men of the Watch Standarte "Feldherrnhalle" are on guard in front of the house. They are a symbol that this house will never be administered in a different way than in the meaning of the fighter whose name it bears.

The way from the National Socialistic combat press to the State press of the Third Reich has been visibly marked by a number of prohibitions, manipulations by the authorities, and the systematical gagging of the right of free speech, which the German democracy had made their rule of life.

Our Party press has become popular under the example of sacrifices. No less than the Führer himself has verified that it has done its part for the final victory of the Movement. Our press had to maintain itself. Self-driven, it had to struggle through prohibitions, harassment and the shameless lies of others to secure its existence. It continued to exist because behind it was not the ordinary "reader-ship", but because the press's business was the

The founder of the paper.
Ten years ago present SA Gruppenführer Josef Berchtold, a young war officer and Führer of the Stosstrupp Adolf Hitler, created the "SA Mann". Berchtold is one of the oldest Party comrades, holds the Blood Order, Coburg Badge, and the Golden Party Honor Badge. Today, among others, he is also assistant editor of "Völkischer Beobachter" in Münich and was the first one to lay the basis for a new form of combat journalism.

business of each Party comrade, each SA Mann, Hitler Youth, man and woman, who frequently purchased our papers with their last pennies and got it on its feet again in the last moment. And finally our press could continue, because it had more people behind it. Herein lies the secret of its success and it thrived. It understood that it had to talk to the people in their language in order to convince them. It attacked and the others had to defend themselves. It could wait if catchwords or slogans were screened. Additionally, our technical means, our style and our phrases were gradually refined, and in numerous variations hammered into people's heads and became more convincing. We called our method combat journalism. We were on the right track.

Has something changed in the meantime? Have we been loyal to our press which made the idealism of its co-fighters the basis of its existence? Many questions are waiting for answers! We would like to show by using the paper serving the Party and the people, which has received a special place in the journalism of the present, that the way, methods and basic elements of our press have remained the same.

In March, 1928 the "SA Mann" was issued for the first time as a monthly addition to the "Völkischer Beobachter", organ of the SA High Command of the NSDAP. A single monthly paper in "VB" format, it was intended to be a journalistic influence for the SA.

The signs of the time showed turmoil. The new edition realized this. Its articles called the best German youth under the flags of the Führer, they want-ed nothing else to rouse them. The slogans were clear.

From top to bottom:
Already the first issue of the "SA Mann" received the trend-setting heading, "Discipline", — Written by 1. Obersten SA-Führers, Hauptmann v. Pfeffer. (the first SA High Leader, Captain v. Pfeffer) - Prior to the prohibition, a prophecy of the Führer. — In such a way, the "SA Mann" was issued under Brüning in the prohibition era. — The new face of the paper since Brüning's fall. — The Stabschef with the Chief of the Press and Propaganda Department, Obersturmbannführer Willi Körbel, who accompanies him on all longer trips. Körbel is solely responsible for the contents of the "SA Mann". Due to his close relationship to the Stabschef, who himself participates in designing the paper, the Kampfblatt (combat paper) always receives the right impulses for processing the major tasks.

"SA Mann - Reich Edition - Vorgis",
is the code which every editor, provided with his
department symbol, puts on the header of the man-
uscript, which here Obertruppführer Horst Apitz
"places into a shooting tube". "In this case, this is
the easiest work", he thinks because he is also the
man for advertising, propaganda, etc.

and completeness of our marvelous National Socialistic Movement to hundreds and thousands of our SA and SS men.

If all of Germany would call the spirit of our SA and SS its own, there would be no more Versailles for our Nation.

You, my comrades, have to mourn numerous dead and tens of thousands of injured; however, if you even only practice the right of self-defense, you go to jail. But nevertheless, you have remained completely loyal to our Movement. Yes, on the contrary, the more National Socialistic men were disowned and

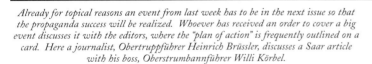

Already for topical reasons an event from last week has to be in the next issue so that the propaganda success will be realized. Whoever has received an order to cover a big event discusses it with the editors, where the "plan of action" is frequently outlined on a card. Here a journalist, Obertruppführer Heinrich Brüssler, discusses a Saar article with his boss, Oberstrumbannführer Willi Körbel.

The small volume and a technically insufficient format were not disturbing. Who would question it!

It could be considered great progress when the edition of January, 1929 could be issued twice a month.

The year 1932 then brought the long-requested expansion to a weekly paper. For three years the "SA Mann" had served the National Socialistic matters in its way and language. Its essays, political discussions, accusations and attacks were supposed to be struggles for the Movement which would fill and overcome the hopelessness of the time with a belief in the future of the youth. The difficulty of the political fight, approaching political decisions and the breakthrough battles of the Party then led to the final expansion of the "SA Mann" into an independent weekly paper. On January 5, 1932 the first paper was issued in the new format. The Führer himself wrote the leading essay in order to give the watchword to his followers. In this key article it was said, according to an analysis of the destruction and the political fall of Germany in the sign of the November Republic of 1918:

"At the moment when especially the SA and the SS had to suffer the most severe injuries and sacrifices, the Reich's Party leadership issues the new SA paper for their manly Party comrades in the SA and SS. It is supposed to strengthen and stabilize the field for the task, the tradition

".....Good. Don't get the page printed yet!"
When the telex from Berlin reports some important news at the last minute, those reports especially "please" the technical operation, which is running like clockwork. Here a new page is set up using pictures. Obertruppführer Elimar-Egmont Roering is telephoning the photo engraver.

suppressed, the bigger became your willingness to sacrifice and the more fanatically you believed!

You have the spirit in you which so far has always been the final winner over foul and shaky systems.

The world around you will go down in shame and our State will become reality! Our new weapon will serve this purpose!"

By this the marching direction was given. The "SA Mann" now used its journalistic methods for the final fight for power. The edition was growing and growing and finally it was in grotesque disproportion considering the number of unemployed within its readers, the SA. In Spring, 1932, Brüning banned the SA. The situation was extremely tense. The prohibition of the SA also naturally paralyzed the newspaper. For the "SA Mann" — organ of the SA High Command of the NSDAP — it therefore overnight became the so-called "Sonntagsbeobachter" (Sunday Observer) with the sub-title Zentralwochenblatt (Central Weekly Paper) of the NSDAP.

In summer the SA prohibition was canceled.

Brüning went to the political desert and found his end there. On August 3, 1932 the "SA Mann" was reissued. The political power struggle was in a decisive phase. Fueled by new power reserves the combat paper of the SA advanced again. Its slogans became sharper and its claims more powerful. Content and technical design were improved. The edition was increasing. Since the foundation of the paper, SA Gruppenführer Josef Berchtold, Führer of Stosstrupp Hitler, was the editor. So to speak, the "SA Mann" was made "voluntarily on the side" as all forces, of course, had to be used in the first place for the "VB". By the end of the year 1932 the "SA Mann" could look back with pride. From an unimportant monthly edition, it had become an important weekly paper with considerable issues.

The National Socialistic press had experienced an unprecedented rise in its intellectual phalanx that was the "SA Mann" and the consequence of its attack then showed the way to a far and only visually felt new future of German journalism. That's why we consider the "SA Mann" to be one of its pioneers.

The new order also gave new form to the press in its political effectiveness. The "SA Mann" stuck to the old proven lines, being convinced that the fight according to new guidelines and other nicer goals, would be continued. Today, the paper is at the top of all German weekly papers, concerning both number issued and content. More than 700,000 papers are issued each week. The new issues required the expansion of the editorship. In Spring, 1936 the Stabschef made the SA Press Chief, Obersturmbannführer Körbel, responsible for the new design. Young editors, some from the old combat press, were utilized for the new work. Editions were created for all twenty-one SA Gruppen, which were issued in periods of 2 to 4 weeks and present to the people the political work of the SA.

However, no paper has such a close relationship to its readers like the millions of readers of the "SA Mann". The ideal fighting community between editors, publishers and readers, has been realized to a high degree.

"SA Mann, Redner (Speaker) and NS Presse stand at the beginning of the Movement", these were the words of the Reichsleiter for the Press, Party Comrade Max Amann, in his report before the Party Congress. This camaraderie made our press great and popular. Also, today it is the visible symbol of the young National Socialistic combat journalism.

The new front of the ideological fight gave a different face to the "SA Mann". Today's "SA Mann" is a first rate combat paper and means of education. And what the Führer prophesied in the first issue has become true. Our State has become a reality.

"Fifteen lines too many"
....said the master of composition (the so-called "Vulture", only by name) to Truppführer Fritz Volkmann after completion of the first page. And then: "To cancel or not to cancel, that is the question!"

"Well, how did we do it?",
Sturmführer Ernst Bayer laughs, former active Sports Trainer and International Supervisor of the overall SA Military Sports.

Well, here it is....
Namely, the latest issue of the "SA Mann", which was just distributed by a promotional campaign. With approximately three-quarter million issues, that is to say approximately 2 million readers, it is leading by far the other political, daily and weekly papers.

TABLE OF CONTENTS

The drawings are by: Elk Eber / O. Flechtner / J. Lazarus - The pictures are by: Ahrens (1) / Bähr (1) / Bibliographisches Institut Leipzig (1) / Bischoff (1) / Bittner (2) / Boegner (12) / van Bosch (1) / Burg (1) / Busch (1) / Büchner (1) / Büsing (1) / Cüpers (1) / DAF., Gaubildstelle Münich (1) / Dähn (2) / Dransfeld (1) / Ehmer (1) / Eisenschink (1) / Engel (2) / Fischer (18) / von Fladung (1) / Fränkische Tageszeitung (1) / Fricke Nachf (47) / Gauarchiv Bayer, Ostmark (1) / Gehlert (1) / Gruppe Hessen (1) / Gruppe Hochland (2) / Gruppe Thüringen (1) / Hauptarchiv (5) / Haymann (2) / Dr. Heck (1) / Hege (1) / Held (1) / Hilz (1) / Hess (1) / Heuer (2) / Hoffmann (39) / Hogefe (1) / Hubmann (3) / Hübner (1) / Jordan (3) / Kaminski (1) / Kassmann (1) / Kester & Co. (1) / Keystone (1) / Knauer (1) / Koch (3) / König (12) / Krauskopf (1) / Krieger (1) / Kurth (1) / Lauterwasser (1) / Lotz (1) / Mathäy (1) / Mauritius (1) / Menzendorf (3) / Metzler (1) / Moisberger (1) / Möbius (8) / Müller (1) / Neubauer (1) / Nortz (1) / NSV. Reichsbildarchiv (7) / OSAF. Archiv (120) / Photothek (1) / Photographen-Innung Berlin (1) / Pinke-pank (1) / Presse-Bild-Zentrale (22) / Presse-Photo (4) / Ramme (1) / Rosenkranz (1) / Röhr (3) / Seiffert (1) / Spieth (2) / Stochus Expressphoto (1) / Scherl (7) / Schirner (5) / Schorer (1) / Transocean (2) / Uhlich (1) / Urbahns (1) / VB.-Bildarchiv (1) / Walz (1) / Wandler (1) / Weber (2) / Wellner (1) / Weltbild (13) / Wiesebach (2) / Winkelmann (1) / Zachger (1)

SAY THANK YOU TO THE SA BY A

DONATION TO THE THANKS OFFERING OF THE NATION

Issued by the order of the SA High Command. Publisher: Franz Eher Nachf. G. m. b. H., Münich 22, Thierschstrasse 11. Chief Editor: Dietrich Loder, Münich; Assistant Editor: Dr. Hans Diebow, Berlin-Charlottenburg: In cooperation with the Department of the Press and Propaganda of the SA. High Command, Obersturmbannführer Willi Körbel. Print: Münich Buchgewerbehaus and Müller & Sohn KG., Münich. Copyright 1938 by Franz Eher Nachf. G. m. b. H., Münich 22. Printed in Germany.